Best Sights to See at
Joshua Tree National Park

By Rob Bignell

Atiswinic Press · Ojai, Calif.

BEST SIGHTS TO SEE AT JOSHUA TREE NATIONAL PARK

A GUIDEBOOK IN THE BEST SIGHTS TO SEE SERIES

Copyright Rob Bignell, 2020

All rights reserved. Except for brief passages quoted in newspaper, magazine, radio, television or online reviews, no portion of this book may be reproduced, distributed, or transmitted in any form by any means, electronic or mechanical, including photocopying, recording, or information storage or retrieval system, without the prior written permission of the author.

Many of the entries in this volume were originally written for and published by the Uken Report. The Uken Report strives to be the most authentic, respected online news and marketing platform in the Coachella Valley. Read it online at ukenreport.com.

Atiswinic Press
Ojai, Calif. 93023
dayhikingtrails.wordpress.com

ISBN 978-1-948872-08-9

Cover design by Rob Bignell
Cover photo of Joshua tree at sunset at Joshua Tree National Park

Manufactured in the United States of America
First printing February 2020

For Kieran
"Follow, follow the sun
And which way the wind blows
When this day is done"
- Xavier Rudd, "Follow the Sun"

Contents

INTRODUCTION   1
Geology   1
Geography   2
History   3
Park Layout   4
How to Get There   7
When to Visit   8
Kids' Activities   10
Tips to Ensure a Safe Hike   11
Maps   14

BEST SIGHTS   17
Granite Monoliths: Skull Rock Trail   19
Joshua Tree Groves: Boy Scout Trail   23
Desert Oases: Fortynine Palms Oasis Trail   27
Ranching History: Barker Dam Nature Trail   32
Rugged Mountains: Lost Horse Mine Trail   35
Sand Dunes: Pinto Basin Sand Dunes Trail   41
Arches: Arch Rock Trail   44
Desert Fauna: Cholla Cactus Garden Trail   48
Night Skies: Porcupine Wash-Ruby Lee Mill Site Trail   51
Desert Wildflowers: West Side Loop   55
Other Park Trails   61

NEARBY TRAILS   63
Big Morongo Canyon Preserve   64

San Gorgonio Mountain	69
San Jacinto Peak	73
Amboy Crater	77
BONUS SECTION I: DAY HIKING PRIMER	**81**
Selecting a Trail	81
Clothing	83
Equipment	85
Navigational Tools	90
Food and Water	92
First-aid Kit	94
Hiking with Children: Attitude Adjustment	96
Family Dog	97
Rules of the Trail	98
Trail Dangers	100
BONUS SECTION II: NATIONAL PARKS PRIMER	**105**
What is (and isn't) a National Park	106
Choosing a Park to Visit	107
Pets	110
Getting Kids Involved	111
Hiking National Parks Tips	112
Services and Amenities	114
Best Sights to See	114

Introduction

Imagine a place where granite monoliths rise out of the ground in fantastical shapes...where otherworldly Joshua trees grow as dense forests...where secluded palm oases beckon weary desert travelers...where the ruins of old ranches and gold mines stand as monuments to men's Herculean efforts and shattered dreams...where bare rugged mountains loom over vast sand dunes...where the Milky Way glitters at night like no man-made light show ever could. The place is real: It's called Joshua Tree National Park.

Located in Southern California, Joshua Tree is an increasingly popular destination for day trippers and tourists alike. But with the park's incredible size of 1,235 square miles and the crowds, how can you ensure that you see its main sights when vacationing or driving through? That's what "Best Sights to See at Joshua Tree National Park" answers. In this volume, we've listed the top 10 most popular sights and detail the top day hiking trails to best experience them.

Geology

For much of Earth's history, the area making up Joshua Tree National Park lay underwater. But there were many eras when it was at the center of the action. Tectonic plates have collided several times where the park now sits, causing granite called gneiss to form beneath the surface.

The park's oldest rocks, Pinto gneiss, are 1.7 billion years old. They can be seen in the Cottonwood, Eagle and Pinto mountains. Another type of gneiss formed about a billion years ago when a vast mountain range rose on the supercontinent Rodinia. Today, that gneiss also can be found in Australia and Antarctica.

The park's most noticeable geological feature – the exposed monzogranite boulders and domes – formed over the past 180 million years as the North American and Pacific tectonic plates slipped past one another. Erosion has removed the rock covering the granite. Some of the exposed boulders are as tall as 20-story buildings and can be seen in the Wonderland of Rocks as well as the Coxcomb, Eagle and Pinto mountains.

Five of the park's six mountains are part of the Transverse Ranges, in which the peaks generally trend east-west. Those ranges – the Cottonwood, Eagle, Hexie, Little San Bernardino, and Pinto – were lifted and compressed by the San Andreas Fault, which runs just south of the park in the Coachella Valley, where Palm Springs is located. Parallel faults run through the park, so earthquakes do occur there. The parks boasts 10 peaks higher than 5000 feet.

Geography

Geographically, the national park is defined by its six mountain ranges with basins in between. Fault lines running through and between these ranges sometimes sport desert oases.

The park sits at the transition line between the Mojave and Colorado (a section of the Sonoran) deserts. It marks the southwestern edge of the Mojave and the western side of the Colorado.

The Mojave Desert is above 3000 feet elevation and makes up the park's northeast section. It's dominated by Joshua trees, the park's namesake, and looks like the desert around Las Vegas.

The Colorado Desert is below 3000 feet and includes the Pinto Basin and park's southeast portion. It is similar in appearance, wildlife, and fauna to the neighboring Coachella Valley and the Phoenix area, the latter sans the saguaro cactus.

History

The area that makes up the modern park has been inhabited for several thousand years. Archeologists know the Pinto Culture hunted game and gathered plants in the area between 8000 and 4000 BCE. Rather than the stark desert it is today, at that time the land was much wetter with trees growing on the mountain sides.

Prior to the arrival of Euro-Americans, the region served as the seasonal home for the Serrano, Cahuilla and Chemehuevi tribes. The Mojave tribe also traveled through the area, using trails between the Colorado River and Pacific Ocean.

Spaniards explored the area in 1772. Mexico, upon gaining independence from Spain, in 1823 sent an expedition there. The region became part of the United States in 1848 following the Mexican-American War.

During the mid-1800s, ranchers arrived and mainly grazed cattle on the desert's tall grasses. They were followed by miners, who between the 1860s and the early 1930s operated several gold, silver and zinc mines. Ranching did not prove profitable in the dry heat, and soon the sparse mineral veins were tapped out.

The advent of the automobile brought day trippers to the desert, however. Thanks to the work of Minerva Hoyt and other activists, the area was named a national monument in 1936.

Its status was upgraded to a national park in 1994. At that time, the park's size also increased by 235,000 square acres.

Today, Joshua Tree receives about a million visitors a year.

Park Layout

The bulk of the park's best sights and the trails to see them are off of the park's main two highways. Park Boulevard loops from the Joshua Tree Visitor Center in Joshua Tree to the Oasis Visitor Center in Twentynine Palms. Pinto Basin Road runs from the Park Boulevard south of the Oasis Visitor Center all the way to the Cottonwood Visitor Center then via Cottonwood Springs Road on to Interstate 10 just west of Chiriaco Summit. A few roads branch off of these two major routes and lead to campgrounds and additional trails.

There are other entry points that offer access to plenty of other interesting sites and trails, however.

From Yucca Valley, Black Rock Canyon Road heads to the Black Canyon Campground and a number of trails in the park's northwest section. Trails leading to South Park Peak also can be accessed from Elata and Warren Vista avenues and from Santa Barbara Drive. Covington Road offers access to Eagle Peak and various hikes. The street Elk Trail connects to a hiking trail that runs to Elata Avenue.

From Twentynine Palms, Indian Cove Road enters the park's northcentral section. It heads to Indian Cove, Rattlesnake Canyon, and the Boy Scout Trail's northern terminus. Fortynine Palms Oasis Road leads to its famous namesake.

Access points also are available on the the park's south side, though none of them are recommended without a 4W drive vehicle or for day trippers. From north of Cactus City east of the Coachella Valley, an unnamed gravel road leads to a trail up Pinkham Canyon. North of Indio, the jeep trail Berdoo Canyon Road heads up the Little San Bernardino Mountains to the Geology Road Tour Road.

There are some access areas to remote areas that are best avoided, unless you're a backcountry backpacker. In the park's

Rugged mountains divide Joshua Tree National Park into several basins. NPS illustration.

northeast central region, Old Dale and Brooklyn Mine roads enter the park several miles east of Twentynine Palms. The same is true for Calif. Hwy. 177, which skirts the park's south-eastern section, and Black Eagle Mountain Road, both near Eagle Mountain.

Overall, about 300 miles of official trails crisscross the park. Many other faint paths, carved out by wildlife and backpackers, exist but are best avoided unless with a local guide or if you are an experienced backcountry hiker.

Arrangement of trails/hikes by road/park layout

As this guidebook focuses on the "best sights to see," the hikes are not arranged by park section or a compass direction. However, all can be found along the park's major roads or ac-

cess points. From west to east, the trails listed in this book appear in the following spatial sequence:
- **Park Boulevard** *(east to west)*
California Riding and Hiking Trail
Contact Mine Trail
Skull Rock Nature Trail
Discovery Trail
Split Rock Loop
Crown Prince Lookout Trail
via Desert Queen Mine Road
  Lucky Boy Vista Trail
  Desert Queen Mine Trail
  Pine City Trail
Ryan Mountain Trail
Ryan Ranch Trail
via Keys View Road (north to south)
  Cap Rock Trail
  California Riding and Hiking Trail
  Lost Horse Mine Trail
  Lost Horse Mine Loop
  Inspiration Peak Trail
  Keys View Trail
via Barker Dam Road (west to east)
  Barker Dam Nature Trail
  Wonderland Wash Trail
  Wall Street Mill Trail
Hidden Valley Nature Trail
Boy Scout Trail (southern terminal)
Willow Hole Trail
Maze Loop
Window Loop (for Window Rock)
- **Pinto Basin Road** *(north to south)*

California Riding and Hiking Trail
Belle's Eye Arch
Arch Rock Trail
Silver Bell Mine Trail
Cholla Cactus Garden Trail
Pinto Basin Sand Dunes Trail
Porcupine Wash-Ruby Lee Mill Site Trail
- **Cottonwood Springs Road** *(south to north)*
Bajada Nature Trail
Cottonwood Spring Trail
Mastodon Peak Trail
Lost Palms Oasis Trail
Victory Palms bushwhack
- **Yucca Valley/Black Rock Canyon Road** *(west/north to east/south)*
South Park Peak Trail
West Side Loop
Hi-View Nature Trail
Panorama Loop
Warren Peak Trail
California Riding and Hiking Trail
- **Twentynine Palms/Indian Cove Road** *(west/north to east/south)*
Boy Scout Trail (northern terminal)
Indian Cove Trail
Fortynine Palms Oasis Trail

How to Get There

Though seemingly remote, Joshua Tree National Park actually is near several large cities and fairly easy to reach.

Most visitors to the national park will travel through or stay in the Palm Springs area, a popular resort destination. In Palm

Springs or the Coachella Valley, get on Interstate 10 and exit onto Calif. Hwy. 62. This takes you directly to the park's major ports of entry.

From Los Angeles and points north, wind your way on the appropriate freeway to I-10 and head east. After crossing the San Gorgonio Pass, exit onto Hwy. 62.

If in San Diego, take Interstate 15 north. At Temecula, go east onto Calif. Hwy. 79, south on Calif. Hwy. 371, and then east onto Calif. Hwy. 74 into Palm Desert. Go straight on Monterey Avenue and then left/west onto I-10. Lastly, exit onto Hwy. 62.

From Phoenix, take I-10 to Palm Springs and exit on Hwy. 62.

If in Las Vegas, take Interstate 15 to Barstow, Calif., then go west onto Interstate 40. Exit onto County Road 66 (aka the National Trails Highway) and at Amboy go right/south onto Amboy Road. In Twentynine Palms, turn left/south onto Goodwin Road and then right/west onto Hwy. 62.

From Flagstaff, Ariz., and Grand Canyon National Park, take Interstate 40 west. Exit onto Kelbaker Road and head south. Turn right/west onto County Road 66. At Amboy, go left/south onto Amboy Road. In Twentynine Palms, turn left/south onto Goodwin Road and then right/west onto Hwy. 62.

Except for the drives from Los Angeles and Palm Springs, visitors will have to cross a lot of desert to reach Joshua Tree. If deserts aren't your thing, then the perceived dullness of the largely flat, monotonous drive will make the otherworldly sights of Joshua Tree all that more thrilling.

When to Visit

The best time to visit Joshua Tree National Park depends upon the season and the time of day.

Fall through spring mark the safest seasons. Summer usually

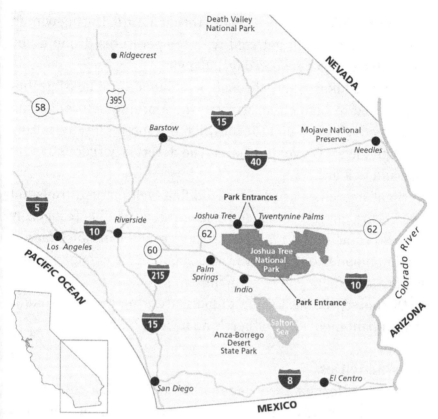

Joshua Tree National Park sits in southern California, east of Los Angeles and north of San Diego. Map not to scale. USGS illustration.

is dangerously hot with an average park temperature of 100 degrees from June through September.

December can be surprisingly chilly, as winter settles over the High Desert; it's much colder than the neighboring Palm Springs and Coachella Valley or the Los Angeles basin. At least a sweatshirt and jacket will be needed from November through January.

Once you've selected the season, consider the time of day for your visit.

Daytime hikes are fine October through April. During winter, however, nights will get cold with temperatures dropping by up to 40 degrees between day and night.

Summer hikes – May through September – are possible, but you'll need to hike either early in the morning before the sun rises too high or at night from when the sun is close to setting through the early evening hours. The desert is gorgeous at sunrise and twilight.

Nighttime hikes are possible on flat, well-marked trails but usually are not recommended elsewhere, as wildlife (especially snakes) come out at night and rocky ground can cause falls. If the full moon is out, however, you should have enough natural light to see where you're stepping.

Of course, the best thing to look at during the nighttime is the brilliant night sky, so there's no need to hike at all.

Kids' Activities

A trip to Joshua Tree National Park can be an educational experience for kids – though they may be having too much fun to even notice that they're learning!

The park delivers a variety of great activities that children can participate in from spring through autumn.

Among the many offerings are ranger-led events. Programs at several locations throughout the park focus on a range of interests, from desert wildlife and plants to preserving local natural and cultural treasures. Check the Joshua Tree National Park website or newspaper for current offerings.

The park also participates in the popular Junior Ranger Kids program. Kids between the ages of 5-13 can become a Junior Ranger. They'll first need to purchase a Junior Ranger booklet (available at any park visitor center) and complete its activities, then they can receive a Junior Ranger badge.

Tips to Ensure a Safe Hike

Joshua Tree National Park is a desert, and unlike the lush woodlands and prairies in other parts of the nation, offers unique hiking challenges. That's no reason to avoid desert trails and all the natural wonders the area offers, but you also should prep for your adventure to ensure your comfort and safety.

Whenever hiking the desert, always consider the following:

• **Clothing** – White and other light colors will better reflect the sunlight than black and dark clothing, which absorb it, resulting in more heat upon the body. Avoid cotton, favoring loose-fitting dry performance shirts. Be sure to don a hat with a brim. A brim provides the extra protection needed to shade your face, not just to avoid sunburn but to prevent being blinded by the sun. Always wear sunglasses with UV protection.

• **Shoes/boots** – You'll want footgear with ankle support, that breathes, and which has a soft, flexible sole to ensure traction. To that end, wear lightweight, permeable hiking boots or hiking shoes. Sandals expose your skin to sunburn, thorns and sharp rocks while running shoes lack the ankle support needed for crossing rocky terrain.

• **Water** – Drink plenty of it but not too much too swiftly or you'll suffer stomach cramps. You'll need at least 2 pints of water per person for every hour on the trail. Consider carrying it in collapsible canteens to lessen the weight. Avoid caffeine before hiking, as that can lead to dehydration. If children accompany you on the hike, get them a hydration pack, which kids are more likely to regularly use as they can more easily sip water as walking.

• **Sunscreen** – An SPF 50 is essential, as sand reflects sunlight back onto the body, resulting in a burn. Sweat will wash away sunscreen, so you likely will need to reapply it during rest breaks. Even if walking through shaded areas, use sunscreen, as the sun is more intense than in northern latitudes.

• **Lip balm** – Lips also can be burned or chapped by sunlight as well as wind. An SPF 30 balm will protect them. Reapply the balm after drinking water.

• **Insect repellent** – Dangerous insects are rare but can be encountered in wet areas such as an oasis or stream. A repellent made with oil of lemon eucalyptus is safest for your skin.

• **Snacks** – Salty snacks are needed to replenish sodium lost while sweating. Sweet snacks most likely will only melt on a hot day.

• **Time of the day** – Mornings almost always are cooler than the afternoon, sometimes by a good 20 degrees, so plan to hike before 10 a.m. Evening hikes after 6 p.m. also are a little cooler than afternoons.

• **Trail difficulty** – If new to hiking, stick to a trail that won't prove too challenging in distance or terrain. The more energy you exert, the more likely you are to overheat.

• **Breaks** – Take more of them, maybe once every 15 minutes, especially if you haven't hiked in a while. This also will give you time to ensure everyone in your hiking party is drinking water and getting a salty snack.

• **Pace** – Reduce your pace to avoid overexertion. You may not cover as much ground as you like, but there are plenty of interesting, short trails to enjoy.

Desert dangers

As a dry, often inhospitable environment, deserts offer both incredible scenic wonders and grave dangers. Because of the former, they make for great hiking terrain…because of the latter, you should be aware of the variety of challenges that you could encounter during a day hike there. Foreknowledge is power.

Among the many risks a desert environment present are:

• **Sun- and heat-related illnesses** – Sun stroke, sunburn, heat stroke, and dehydration are serious, life-threatening ailments that often affect hikers who don't respect the desert. Hiking during more temperate seasons and hours of the day, drinking plenty of water, dressing properly, using sunscreen, and pacing oneself all can go a long way to avoiding these problems.

• **Flashfloods** – Often trails head down canyons and arroyos, which are perfect spots to get caught in a flashflood. When hiking in such locations, always keep an eye out for an escape route to higher ground. Also keep an ear out for a roar rising in volume up canyon, even on sunny days, as thunderstorms several miles away can quickly send floodwater roiling down a canyon or a dry run. If you hear such a sound, immediately head to higher ground.

• **Creepy crawlies** – Spiders, scorpions and snakes all can sting or bite, and some are poisonous. To avoid meeting one, don't place your hand in holes or pick up rocks where these creatures like to hide and don't place your feet in grass or brush where you can't see your toes. Should you encounter one, keep your distance and slowly back away.

• **Getting overadventurous** – Exploring side canyons that you don't have maps for or climbing up rocks and cliff sides that have no easy way down are all no-no's in the desert. You don't want to get lost or become trapped so that your water supplies run out before you can be rescued.

Of all of these dangers, sun- and heat-related illnesses by far are the most common followed by injuries from climbing where one shouldn't and getting lost by going off the trail. I've spent several years hiking the Colorado, Mojave, Sonoran, Chihuahuan and Great Basin deserts, and during all of that time have encountered one rattlesnake, one scorpion, and zero flashfloods. What's even better is you can prevent sun- and heat-related illnesses and being overadventurous simply by using common sense.

Reducing impact on a desert environment
With so little rainfall, deserts are a delicate, fragile environment. The limited number of plants and animals residing in the national park can be deeply affected by even minor changes.

To limit the impact of your hike upon the desert, stick to these simple practices:

• **Leave what's natural in its place** – Uprooting plants and moving rocks actually disturbs food and shelter sources for desert animals.

• **Walk single file** – Doing so restricts the impact of your footsteps to a single narrow path. Stepping off a path can dislodge plant roots, compress soil, or shift rocks about.

• **Carry out your leftovers** – Rather than decompose, food tossed to the ground often will mummify. Since human foods (such as oranges and bananas) usually aren't native to deserts, seeing a mummified peeling looks out of place. All other garbage, such as wrappers, should be carried out as well.

• **Keep noise down** – Our shouts carry farther in the open desert and echo off rock canyon walls, stressing animals and diminishing the experience for other hikers.

Maps

To properly prepare for any hike, you should examine maps before hitting the trail and bring them with you (See Bonus Section I for more.). No guidebook can reproduce a map as well as the aerial pictures or topographical maps that you can find online for free. To that end, Printable maps showing hiking trails, campgrounds, parking lots and other facilities for the trails listed in this book are available online at *dayhikingtrails.wordpress.com/trail-maps/#joshuatree.*

Best Sights

Joshua Tree National Park is so vast that unless you spend years there, you won't see all it offers. So when you have only a few days at best to visit the park, what are the absolute must-see sights? Following are the park's 10 best features and the day hiking trails for getting to them.

Wind, rain and the freezing-thawing cycle has carved a skull-like formation in Joshua Tree National Park. NPS photo.

Granite Monoliths
Skull Rock Trail

Families can day hike with their children to Skull Rock – not the one in Neverland of "Peter Pan" fame but one bearing an uncanny resemblance.

The Skull Rock Trail runs 1.75-miles round trip, heading through the famous Jumbo Rocks, a collection of massive, rounded granite rocks that many park visitors often scramble over.

Spring and fall mark the best time to hike the loop if only because temperatures will be most comfortable. Early morning right after dawn and late afternoon just before dusk offer the best lighting.

To reach the trail, take Calif. Hwy. 62 on the park's north side. Use the north entrance, which is in Twentynine Palms, three miles south of the junction of Hwy. 62 and Utah Trail. The trailhead is on Park Boulevard, which is the park's main east-west road. Look for the roadside parking area immediately north of Jumbo Rocks Campground.

Though Skill Rock is within sight of the roadside parking area, explore the Jumbo Rocks first. So head west onto the trail, walking away from Skull Rock. Hikers' feet over the decades have nicely compacted the trail's sandy surface.

You'll pass through a narrow canyon in which some of the boulders of Jumbo Rock rise about you. Though seemingly desolate from a distance, these clusters nicely capture the desert's scarce rain and create a number of micro-climates for varied plants and animals. Among the latter who find plenty of food here are bobcats, coyotes, chuckwallas, great horned owls, jackrabbits, snakes, and wood rats.

The slot canyon opens onto a wash. Plants you'll spot here are the park's namesake, the Joshua tree, cacti, cholla, creosote, jojoba, juniper, Mojave yucca, nolina, oak, paperbag bush, and pinyon.

After the wash, the trail comes to the base of another surreal boulder pile. The slabs in this area formed below the earth's surface as tectonic movement heated the rock. As melting, it rose upward until cooling just below the surface. Called monzogranite, wind and rain eventually exposed them and further cracked their joints while shaping and rounding them.

Upon reaching Park Boulevard, cross at the walkway and follow the paved campground road west. There are limited facilities here, should you need them. When the campground road splits, go left then on the new road take the second left. The trail leaves the campground just before you crest this small loop.

Your route veers toward the Park Boulevard then wraps around the base of more boulder piles in Jumbo Rocks. Amid them, you'll soon come across the rock formation appropriately named Skull Rock.

When this slab of granite was exposed to the open air, two depressions existed where the formation's hollowed eye sockets are. Rain drops accumulated in these depressions, eroding away more granite. As the depressions grew in size, so did the amount of accumulating rain, speeding up the erosion. Wind and rain meanwhile rounded the "head" above the eyes.

Continuing past the formation, take the trail to Park Boulevard. Cross at the walkway back to your vehicle. On the drive out, stop at the Oasis Visitor Center for some great displays and exhibits about the park's geology, flora and fauna.

Lastly, some safety notes: Most of the hike is in the open sun, so be sure to lather on the sunscreen, wear a sunhat and sunglasses, and to carry extra water. If scrambling over the rocks, be sure to keep your balance (the fall is a hard one) and never place your hands or feet into a crevice where you can't see them, as there could be snakes resting there.

Other Trails to Granite Monoliths

Clusters of monzogranite boulders form fascinating sights and mazes all throughout the national park. Besides being fun to clamber over and around, some of them appear in unique shapes that fire the imagination.

Among the best trails to explore the park's granite monoliths are:

• **Boy Scout Trail** – You can hike deep into the Wonderland of Rocks on this 8-mile one-way trail. Always stay within sight of the trail so you do not get lost among the boulders. If doing only part of the trail, the south trailhead off of Park Boulevard is preferred to the north trailhead at Indian Cove. Should you do the entire length, park rangers strongly advise using a vehicle shuttle.

• **Cap Rock Trail** – The 0.4-mile loop circles the fascinating Cap Rock formation, which is surrounded by Joshua trees and desert fauna. The Cap Rock parking area is at the junction of Park Boulevard and Keys View Road.

• **Discovery Trail** – A new trail made for kids, the flat 0.7-mile loop heads through gigantic rocks over desert washes while linking to Skull Rock and Split Rock Loop trails at Face Rock. Start at the Skull Rock parking area east of Jumbo Rocks Campground on Park Boulevard.

• **Hidden Valley Nature Trail** – The 1-mile loop heads to a rock-enclosed valley at the park's "center" off of Park Boulevard. Cattle rustlers allegedly used the valley. Park at the Hidden Valley picnic area.

• **Indian Cove Nature Trail** – A great trail for climbing boulders, the 0.6-mile kid-friendly loop passes yucca and various small wildflowers. Pick up the trail at the Indian Cove Campground at the end of Indian Cove Road.

• **Split Rock Loop** – Face Rock, the Jumbo Rocks, and even wildflowers await on this 2.5-mile loop. It starts at the Split Rock picnic area near Park Boulevard.

• **Willow Hole Trail** – The 6.8-mile round trip trail, which begins on the Boy Scout Trail's southern end, heads along and then enters the Wonderland of Rocks. It ends at a group of willow trees.

• **Wonderland Wash Trail** – Explore the impressive Wonderland of Rocks on your way to the Wonderland Ranch ruins on this 2.1-mile trail. It ends at the prominent Astro Dome rock formation. The trailhead is the same as the one for the Wall Street Mill Trail off of Park Boulevard.

Joshua Tree Groves

Boy Scout Trail (southern trailhead)

Day hikers can enjoy a walk through a large Joshua tree forest via a segment of the Boy Scout Trail. The trail runs through a grove for a 2.4-mile round trip. To reach the trailhead, from Calif. Hwy. 62 in Joshua Tree, go right/south onto Park Boulevard (in town, aka Quail Springs Road). After the park's western entrance station, drive for several miles then turn into the Boy Scout Trailhead parking lot on the road's left/north side; the lot is just past the Quail Springs Picnic Area.

This marks the trail's southern terminus. The trail heads north into the desert. To the east, San Gorgonio Mountain looms on the horizon, though it's several miles distant.

After crossing a couple of washes and swerving northeast, the trail ascends into a Joshua tree forest. The park's namesake are gigantic members of the lily family, so named because their outstretched branches reminded Mormon pioneers of the Biblical figure Joshua calling out God.

Joshua trees can be found all across the Mojave Desert in California, Arizona, Nevada and Utah; indeed, some biologists suggest that the Mojave can be defined as the range of Joshua trees. The Joshua trees primarily grow between 1,300 and 5,900 feet elevation, though, so they won't be found on the desert's mountain tops or its low areas, such as those in Death Valley.

For desert plants, Joshua trees are fast growers. They can rise 3 inches a year for their first decade. Barring a natural calamity, the trees survive hundreds of years. The oldest ones here are thought to be about 10 centuries old; when they were seedlings, the Anasazi were building their cliff dwellings and Leif Eriksson was sailing for North America.

Otherworldly in appearance, Joshua trees can grow up to 15 feet high. They often clump together as sprouting from a parent rootstalk.

If hiking the trail between February and late April, you might spot the Joshua Tree in bloom. Its creamy white flowers are about 1-3 inches long. Joshua trees don't bloom every year, though; first a winter freeze and then just the right amount of rain must fall.

Though it looks like a tree, the Joshua tree is one in name only. It's actually a type of yucca, which is part of the lily family.

You may want to soon hike the trail while the Joshua tree is still around. Scientists predict climate change will reduce its range by 90 percent before the end of this century. If that occurs, the national park's ecosystems will change dramatically.

A split appears in the Boy Scout Trail as approaching a small, crescent-shaped butte. Veer right/northeast to stay on the main trail.

After passing the butte, the trail continues northeast toward the basin's eastern edge. Small mounds of monzogranite boulder rise amid the Joshua tree forest.

At 1.2 miles, the hike reaches a side trail going right/northeast to Willow Hole. That trail heads into the rock formations forming the basin's east wall and is known for its washes and wind-sculpted boulder formations. This marks a good spot to turn back.

If feeling more adventurous, you can continue on the Boy Scout Trail. The path runs for another 6.8 miles round into the hills ahead, then descends to a basin floor, ending at Indian Cove Road near Twentynine Palms.

The trail is entirely open to the sun, so be sure to don a brimmed hat, sunglasses and sunscreen, as well as bring plenty of water.

Large Joshua tree groves flourish along the southern part of the Boy Scout Trail. NPS photo.

Other Trails to Joshua Tree Groves

Joshua Tree National Park's namesake aren't really trees at all. Instead, these gigantic members of the lily family, so named because their outstretched branches reminded Mormon pioneers of the Biblical figure Joshua calling out God. Walking through a forest of them is a surreal experience and feels like you're on another planet.

Among the best trails to explore the park's Joshua tree groves are:

• **Cap Rock Trail** – The 0.4-mile trail loops through Joshua trees as circling the fascinating Cap Rock formation. The Cap Rock parking area is at the junction of Park Boulevard and Keys View Road.

• **Hi-View Nature Trail** – This 1.3-mile loop heads up a ridge for a panoramic view of a Joshua tree grove. Benches are

available for sitting. Park in the lot at the end of South Park Road in Yucca Valley.
- **Indian Cove Trail** – Kids will appreciate this short and easy 0.6-mile hike that offers plenty of opportunities for boulder climbing. The trailhead is at the end of Indian Cove Road West, which is accessible from Twentynine Palms.
- **Maze Loop** – Forests of Joshua trees, as well as monolithic rocks, slot canyons with high rock walls, and the famous Window Rock formation, await on this 4.7-miles hike. It leaves from Park Boulevard.
- **Panorama Loop** – The 6.6-mile trail runs along a ridgeline in the Little San Bernardino Mountains as heading through a dense Joshua tree forest and a pinyon-juniper woodland while gaining 1100 feet in elevation. Park at and leave from the Black Rock Nature Center.
- **West Side Loop** – Joshua trees abound on the ridges and washes along this 4.7-mile loop. Leave from the west side of Black Rock Campground after parking at the nature center there.
- **Willow Hole Trail** – The 6.8-mile round trip trail, which starts on the Boy Scout Trail's southern terminus, heads through a Joshua tree forest and alongside the Wonderland of Rocks. It ends at a group of willow trees.

Desert Oases
Fortynine Palms Oasis Trail

Day hikers can head to a secluded oasis on the Fortynine Palms Oasis Trail.

The 2.8-mile round trip trail offers a number of panoramic views and the chance to see desert plants and wildlife. It sports a 350-foot elevation gain.

To reach the trailhead, from Calif. Hwy. 62 in Twentynine Palms, turn right/south onto Canyon Road. As the street curves east, it becomes Fortynine Palms Canyon Road. This is an access road into the north end of the national park with no ranger station. Theoretically, you don't have to pay park admission to hike this trail, but your vehicle can be cited for not having a park pass should a ranger come by. The road ends at a parking lot with the trailhead leaving from the southeast corner.

A single track of sand and gravel heads uphill through the often barren and rocky landscape. Stone stairs along the way help your ascend and descend the ridgelines. Sections of the trail are an old Native American path that led from the desert to the oasis spring.

Red barrel cacti be seen alongside the trail. The most common of the cylindrical cacti, their color ranges from deep red to white and yellow with all shades in-between. Older red barrel cacti tend to lean toward the southwest.

Brittlebrush clusters also thrive trailside. They can grow to almost five feet high. Their leaves are quite fragrant, and early Spanish missions in this part of the world used to burn their sap as incense.

During spring, you can enjoy a lot of cacti and wildflower blossoms, especially after a rainfall. Both the red barrel cactus and the brittlebush bloom a brilliant yellow.

There are no Joshua trees, the park's namesake, on this trail, though. The elevation in this part of the park is a bit too high for them.

You'll also spot a number of small, harmless lizards scurrying about and sunbathing near the trail. The Western side-blotched lizard likes open ground exposed to the sun, especially where there's rock and loose soil. The Great Basin collared lizard usually sticks to rocky slopes.

Quails also can be seen, though they are rarer. The plump Gambel's quail is about the size of a soccer ball and well-camouflaged. Males, however, have a cream-colored belly with black patch. Their calls are a common sound in Southwestern deserts. In spring, males make a *kaa* sound to signal they're seeking a mate. When quails notice you, they'll probably chirp *chip-chip-chip*, which tells the rest of their covey that something suspicious is nearby.

Desert tortoises are rarer still. If you spot a hole next to a creosote bush, the national park's lone species of tortoise might be nearby. Only able to move a mere 0.2 miles per hour – or about as fast as traffic on a Los Angeles freeway during rush hour – tortoises construct up to 30 feet of dens underground. They are a threatened species, so should you see one, stay clear; if frightened, they will void their bladder, which diminishes their chances of retaining enough water to survive the desert's dryness.

At 0.75 miles, the trail descends toward the oasis. Along the way, you'll be treated to scenic views looking across Fortynine Palms Canyon.

About 0.8 miles in marks the trail's highest point. Keep walking, and like a desert mirage, the oasis seemingly pops out on the horizon.

California fan palms rise between boulders that shade a

Several oases, including Fortynine Palms, dot Joshua Tree National Park. NPS photo.

trickling spring and its pool (which sometimes goes dry). Songbirds flock here, especially orange and black orioles who feed on the ripe berry-like fruit of the palm tree.

Three different orioles are common in the national park – the hooded, Bullock's, and Scott's. The skull cap and breast of the male hooded oriole is a bright orange while the Bullock's oriole is a mix of black and orange. The Scott's oriole has a black head and yellow breast. All are migrants through the park.

Bring a picnic lunch as well to enjoy under the palm canopy.

The oasis (and trail) is closed at night so local wildlife can access the spring. Both sheep and coyotes come here, and the following day you may see their tracks on the sand around the palms.

A spring exists at Fortynine Palms because fault lines force underground water to the surface. Miners planted the palms to mark the spring's location.

The trail is best avoided during summer heat, so limit its use to October through June. There's no shade except at the oasis. Regardless the time of the year, bring plenty of water. Lastly, the trail can be slick after a rain.

Other Trails to Desert Oases

What would a desert be without an oasis? Sitting in the Mojave Desert, Joshua Tree has six. The California fan palm oases usually occur along fault lines.

You can discover the park's other desert oases on these trails:

• **Cottonwood Spring Trail** – This brief 0.2-mile round trip walk heads to a fan palm oasis with cottonwood trees. It's a great spot to see a variety of birds and on top of that, there's shade! About 24 palms were planted here in the 1890s because of a once active spring. The trailhead is 1 mile east of the Cottonwood Visitor Center.

• **Lost Palms Oasis Trail** – This 7.2-mile round trip backcountry hike heads to a remote oasis in a shady canyon. Dike Springs is in a side canyon but requires some bouldering to reach. Park in the Cottonwood Spring lot.

• **Oasis of Mara Trail** – An easy 0.5-mile loop, the oasis has a long history of being used by Native Americans and wildlife. Leashed pets are allowed on the trail. The trailhead is at the Oasis Visitor Center.

• **Victory Palms bushwhack** – After taking in the Lost Palms Oasis, continue down canyon for a mile. Only a half-dozen palms stand in the oasis. It's a 9.2-mile round trip backcountry hike that requires bouldering.

A sixth oasis, in **Munsen Canyon**, has no trail to it. An arduous cross-country, 9-mile one-way hike up a wash and boulder-strewn canyon in the Eagle Mountains reaches it. A set of eight small groves sit in a two-mile stretch of the canyon.

Ranching History
Barker Dam Nature Trail

Day hikers can enjoy a lake created more than a century ago in the national park.

The 1.5-mile round trip Barker Dam Nature Trail is like a sampler plate of all the national park offers – monolithic rock mounds, historic sites, desert with iconic Joshua trees, and Native American petroglyphs.

To reach the trailhead, take Park Boulevard into the park. Near the Hidden Valley Campground area, go northeast onto Barker Dam Road. In just under two miles, turn left/north into the Barker Dam Nature Trail parking lot.

The stem to the lollipop trail heads northwest from the lot into the desert. A sand trail, it crosses a couple of dry washes and approaches two large mounds of boulders. The loop begins at their base; go right/counterclockwise on the loop. This heads between the mounds and requires some walking over the rocks.

The outcroppings are called inselbergs. Made of monzonite, groundwater shaped the one-time rectangular rocks by eroding their corners. Wind, the rare rainfall, freezing and thawing further rounded, shaped and cracked the huge mounds.

Upon passing through the boulders, the trail reaches a small blue lake. In an effort to collect and preserve the scarce water, ranchers long ago built rainwater catchments called "tanks." Today, this tank serves as a small oasis with willow trees. Birds, frogs and mosquitoes are common at the lake in March. Throughout the day, the water reflects the rock mounds while sunset casts them in a beautiful array of colors.

After taking in the lake, continue walking west along the shoreline. The trail quickly arrives at Barker Dam (sometimes

For decades, ranchers tried to tame the desert that is now Joshua Tree National Park, including building a dam to water their livestock. NPS photo.

referred to as Big Horn Dam), which holds the lake water in place.

Miner and cattleman C. O. Barker built the original nine-foot-high Barker Dam in 1900. Nearly a half-century later in 1949, rancher William "Bill" Keys raised the dam by six feet. Other catchments or their remnants, including White Tank, can be found in the area.

The trail next curves southeast through open desert. Joshua trees dot the plain.

Along the way is a short stem trail to ancient Cahuilla petroglyphs and pictographs. Unfortunately, in 1961, a Walt Disney crew, while filming "Chico, the Misunderstood Coyote," painted over some of them so they would appear brighter; because of that, today some of them appear garish and unnatural, so they sometimes are referred to as the "Disney petroglyphs." Most of the petroglyphs are of geometric shapes and stick figures.

At the next intersection, turn left/east. This follows the side of a rock mound and then cuts between two of them.

Along the way, watch for the Mojave mound cactus, whose flowers sprout a brilliant red each spring. A type of hedgehog cactus, it thrives in the rocky terrain around Joshua trees.

Once at the stem trail, go right/southeast and retrace your steps to the parking lot.

Other Trails to Ranch Ruins

Despite that the desert receives less than 10 inches of rain a year, settlers tried decades ago to farm it. At least in what is now Joshua Tree National Park, those efforts at ranching and homesteading by and large failed. Still, remnants of their efforts on such marginal land holdings remain a testament to their rugged individualism.

Among the best trails to explore the park's ranching history:

• **Hidden Valley Nature Trail** – The 1-mile trail doesn't lead to a ranch but to a 55-acre box canyon allegedly used by cattle rustlers, the McHaney Gang. The best time to hike this trail off of Park Boulevard is early morning and late afternoon, as it will be crowded at midday.

• **Ryan Ranch Trail** – The easy 1-mile round trip trail heads along an old ranch road to a century-old adobe homestead. See if you can spot a bright sheen on the adobe bricks, as they were constructed with gold dust from a local mine. The trailhead is off of Park Boulevard east of the road to Ryan Campground.

• **Wonderland Wash Trail** – Discover the Wonderland Ranch ruins after passing through the impressive Wonderland of Rocks on this 2.1-mile trail. The trailhead is the same as that for the Wall Street Mill Trail off of Park Boulevard.

Rugged Mountains
Lost Horse Mine Trail

Stark, rock-strewn mountains rise all across California's deserts thanks to the Pacific and North American tectonic plates colliding. A good place to explore those peaks in the national park is on the Lost Horse Mine Trail.

A 4-mile round trip segment of the trail heads to the base of one desert summit – Lost Horse Mountain, which rises nearly a mile above sea level to 5,278 feet.

To reach the trailhead, from Calif. Hwy. 62 in Joshua Tree, turn right/south onto Park Boulevard (aka Quail Springs Road) into the national park. Just before Cap Rock, go right/south onto Keys View Road. Next, turn left/southeast onto Lost Mine Road, which quickly becomes gravel. A parking lot is at the road's end, and the trail heads out from the lot's southeast corner.

The route immediately enters a low-lying arm of the Little San Bernardino Mountains. A stout range, the Little San Bernardinos run about 40 miles along the Coachella Valley's northeast side. The mountains mark the transition zone between the valley's Colorado Desert environment and the Mojave Desert that sits above the coastal basin.

About 2 million years ago, the Little San Bernardinos began to rise, thanks to action along the San Andreas Fault where the North American and Pacific tectonic plates slip against one another. Just about every time there's an earthquake in the neighboring Coachella Valley, the Little San Bernadinos grow a bit taller.

The rocks making up the mountains are mainly granitic and metamorphic and are hundreds of millions of years old. Granitic rock forms when magma solidifies underground; the coarse rock usually contains a large amount of quartz. Metamorphic rock also forms underground but when heat and pressure alters the chemical composition of other rocks, such as sandstone or shale.

Joshua trees and yucca line much of the boulder-strewn trailsides. You'll gain about 500 feet of elevation on a gradual uphill grade.

About 1.8 miles in, a spur off the trail heads to Lost Horse Mine. The rusted remnants of its stamp mill mark the mine's entry. A chain-linked fence prevents hikers from walking amid the mill and entering the mine, however.

For two decades beginning in 1884, miners pulled gold and silver from the mountainside. About 16,000 ounces of silver and 10,000 ounces of gold were extracted. That may not seem like much, but in today's dollars it's nearly $5 million of gold.

The trail and mine got its name because one of the mine's original owners had lost his horse while camping in the area. That's when he met a man who told him about finding the gold and sold him his claim to it for $1000.

The Lost Horse Mine Trail actually is a loop through the mountains and from the spur heads south. Rather than take that long circle route, which adds 2.9 miles to your hike, instead retrace your steps to the parking lot.

The entire route is exposed to the sun, so be sure to don sunscreen, sunglasses and a hat as well as bring plenty of water.

Other Trails up Rugged Mountains

Several minor mountain ranges divide Joshua Tree National Park into a series of desert basins. Though they appear desolate and foreboding in the hot sun, many miners often clambered about these ranges looking for gold, silver and other minerals that would make them rich. Today, the rocky mountains offer the wealth of beautiful and spectacular vistas.

The ruins of old mines and equipment, such as those at Lost Horse Mine, are strewn across Joshua Tree National Park. NPS photo.

The best trails to explore the park's rugged mountains include:

• **Lost Horse Mine Loop** – You'll gain 550 feet in elevation from some great views on this 6.5-mile loop. The trailhead is at the end of Lost Horse Mine Road, which branches from Keys View Road.

• **Inspiration Peak Trail** – This 1.2-mile round trip hike from Keys View offers fantastic views of the Coachella Valley and the Salton Sea. The summit is at 5,550-feet.

• **Mastodon Peak Trail** – This 3-mile loop in the park's southeastern section is perfect at sunset as the rocks glow orange in the dimming light. Reaching the craggy granite summit requires an off-trail rock scramble. The trailhead is in the

Cottonwood Spring parking area with a 375-foot change in elevation; some maps refer to it as the Mastodon Mine Loop Trail.

• **Panorama Loop** – The 6.6-mile trail gains 1,100 feet in elevation as heading up a wash along a ridgeline in the Little San Bernardino Mountains, offering plenty of scenic views. Park at and leave from the Black Rock Nature Center.

• **Ryan Mountain Trail** – An excellent spot to enjoy either sunrise or sunset, the trail runs 3-mile round trip to a 5,457-foot summit with 360 degree views. Along the 1050-foot climb, the Hall of Horrors rock area and Saddle Rock can be seen from above. The trailhead is off of Park Boulevard between Sheep Pass and Ryan campgrounds.

• **South Park Peak Trail** – The 0.6-mile loop heads up to a peak overlooking Yucca Valley with great views of San Gorgonio Mountain and San Jacinto Peak. The sunsets here are spectacular. Though technically not in the national park, it is accessed via the park's Black Rock Canyon Campground.

• **Warren Peak Trail** – The reward for this 6.2-mile round trip with 1,100 feet in elevation gain are the incredible views of San Jacinto Peak and San Gorgonio Mountain. Do the hike in spring when Joshua Tree's temperatures are pleasant but the two peaks are snow-capped. Park at and leave from the Black Rock Nature Center.

Other Trails to Historic Mining Sites

Joshua Tree's rugged mountains vibrate with a rich history of mining. From the 1800s to the Great Depression in what is now the park, there were 300 mines, though few were profitable. The ruins of several of those mines and their abandoned machinery dot the landscape. While hiking to these sites is fine, never enter any of the mines and do not touch rusted metal or other artifacts.

Among the best trails for discovering those ruins are:
- **Contact Mine Trail** – The short 3.9-miles round trip heads 700 feet up an old mountain road to a mountainside mine with rusting machinery. The trailhead leaves from Park Boulevard south of the Twentynine Palms entrance station.
- **Desert Queen Mine Trail** – Until 1961, gold pulled from the mine shafts here supplied the Wall Street Mill. The 4.9-mile round trip hike is largely flat then crosses a canyon to the mine ruins.
- **Lost Horse Mine Loop** – The best spot in the park to see a mine and mill is the Lost Horse Mine on this trail. The hike from the the trailhead off of Lost Horse Mine Road, a branch of Keys View Road, runs 4-mile round trip, but doing the whole 6.5-mile loop allows you to also see the unsuccessful Optimist Mine, where only a stone chimney remains.
- **Lucky Boy Vista Trail** – This easy 2.5-mile round trip trail gains 125 feet elevation on its way to an old mine and the overlook at it. The trailhead is off of Desert Queen Mine Road north of Park Boulevard.
- **Mastodon Peak Trail** – A 3-mile loop climbs 375 feet almost to the top of the granite peak then past an old gold mine. The trail leaves from the Cottonwood Springs parking area near Pinto Basin Road; some maps refer to it as the Mastodon Mine Loop Trail.
- **Moortens Mill Trail** – The 1.2-mile round trip trail heads up 154 feet to the Moortens Mill Site. It branches off the Mastodon Peak Trail. It recently washed out and as of this writing remains closed pending repair.
- **Porcupine Wash-Ruby Lee Mill Site Trail** – The ruins of a well and mill site sit along the northern leg of this 8.8-miles loop at the base of the Hexie Mountains. Pickup the trail from the parking area on Pinto Basin Road.

- **Silver Bell Mine Trail** – Two wooden structures and a few artifacts remain at the filled-in entries to Silver Bell Mine on this 1.3-mile round trip trail. The trailhead is at a pullout on Pinto Basin Road; look for the "Exhibit Ahead" sign at Pinto Basin's northwest end.
- **Wall Street Mill Trail** – A well-preserved mill used to refine mined gold sits at the end of this 2.4-mile round trip trail off of Queen Valley Road, which connects to Park Boulevard. It was used during the early 1930s during a second gold rush at Joshua Tree.

Sand Dunes

Pinto Basin Sand Dunes Trail

What would a desert be without oases and sand dunes? At Joshua Tree National Park, you can hike to both ... sort of.

Joshua Tree has a few oases, of which 49 Palms Oasis is the most famous and the easiest to reach. And then there are the Pinto Basin Sand Dunes.

They technically aren't dunes but a layer of fine sand covering an elevated ridge.

No marked trail heads to the dunes, but they're visible from Turkey Flats and can be reached with a 3.94-miles round trip north-northeast cross-country walk.

To reach the trailhead, from the park's Oasis Visitor Center on Utah Trail just south of Calif. Hwy. 62, take the former south. Once in the park, Utah Trail becomes Park Boulevard. Turn left/southeast onto Pinto Basin Road. In a little more than 12 miles, look for the Pinto Basin Sand Dunes Trailhead on the road's left/north side. Park in the lot.

A trail that used to be an old road at the lot's north end heads across Turkey Flats for about 400 feet to a borrow pit. It's a man-made feature where material was excavated for use at another location.

You don't have to stop hiking there, though. The rest of the way to the dunes requires some bushwhacking, and you'll gain about 65 feet in elevation along the way.

Begin by heading back to the parking lot. Then walk in a straight line on a bearing of 34 degrees. (Yes, you should carry a compass when day hiking!) Prominent on the horizon is Pinto Mountain, a 3,987-foot summit.

This bearing crosses Turkey Flats, so named because allegedly a farmer bought the land in the 1920s with the intention of setting up a turkey farm there. Reality soon sunk in, so no

Joshua Tree National Park doesn't actually have sand dunes, just layers of sand over ridges that create the appearance of dunes. NPS photo.

turkey farm was built, but the name stuck. Creosote Flats – as creosote is the dominant plant here – would be more fitting.

The route heads up a "dune," though you'll be able to tell that you're just on a ridge as rocky outcroppings rise out of the sand.

Another giveaway that you're not on a dune are diminutive wildflowers that bloom in spring. Both violet-colored desert sand verbena and pink desert calico blossoms can be seen, and neither would be able to root in shifting sand.

One thing you won't see in the basin is the Joshua tree. At a lower elevation than the park's northwestern portion, Pinto Basin sits in the Sonoran Desert where Joshua trees don't grow.

Some 6000 to 10,000 years ago, the basin was far less foreboding; in fact, it was downright inviting. Creeks flowed off the surrounding forested mountains with a waterway heading through the basin's center. Hunter-gatherers, named "Pinto Man" by modern archeologists, flourished here.

At about 1 mile in, you'll crest the ridge. Stay on a 34 degrees bearing, and in 0.9 miles, you'll reach a drop-off, where the ridge falls 100 feet into the Pinto Wash. This marks a good spot to turn back.

The entire hike is exposed to the sun, so be sure to don sunscreen, sunglasses and sunhat as well as carry plenty of water. As you're slogging across sand, you'll definitely want to wear quality hiking boots and use a trekking pole. To avoid heat stroke, the trail is best done during February to April and October to November when temperatures are pleasant.

If hiking in a group, walk single file to minimize impact on the terrain; a number of animals make their homes here by burrowing, and walking on the desert can pack the soil or cover openings with sand.

Note: You can shorten the route by 0.14 miles by skipping the road to the borrow pit or by 1.8 miles if you only walk to where the dune – er, ridge – crests.

Arches

Arch Rock Trail

Day hikers can head to an arch sculpted by Mother Nature out of granite.

The 1.3-mile lollipop Arch Rock Trail partially explores the granite rock formations surrounding White Tank Campground.

To reach the trailhead, from the park's Oasis Visitor Center on Utah Trail just south of Calif. Hwy. 62, take the former south. Once in the park, Utah Trail becomes Park Boulevard. Turn left/southeast onto Pinto Basin Road. In about 2.2 miles, look for a parking lot on the road's right/west side. Park in the lot.

The trail leaves from the lot's south side, crossing desert as paralleling Pinto Basin Road. During spring, especially after a rainfall, wildflowers bloom along the trail. A variety of cacti can be seen year around.

At 0.15 miles, the route junctions with the California Riding and Hiking Trail. Go left/east onto the new trail and cross Pinto Basin Road. After doing so, turn right/southeast onto the Arch Rock Trail.

The trail gently descends on its way to White Tank Campground.

At 0.55 miles in, the route reaches its loop portion. Go right/southwest onto the loop. Two other trails branch off the loop, both to the campground. The second of those branches also is named Arch Rock Trail, for the convenience of campers. Don't turn onto the branching trails but stay on the loop.

The third branching trail, at about 0.67 miles in, is a stem leading to Arch Rock. Turn right/southeast onto it.

You'll be treated a side view of Arch Rock, which spans about 30 feet. Taking a few steps off the main trail allows you to get underneath it, and the surrounding rocks can be climbed

Though small, a number of arches – most notably Arch Rock – can be found across Joshua Tree National Park. NPS photo.

so you even can touch the arch.

The rocks here are White Tank Granite and composed of three types of minerals. The clear, glass-like rock is quartz, the milky white mineral is feldspar, and the flaky black stone is biotite.

They formed between 135-155 million years ago when magma pushed up into the overlying rock then cooled and hardened. Since then, the overlying rock has eroded away, exposing the granite. Once above ground, rain and wind eroded a hole within the rock slab while rounding its top, resulting in an arch.

There are several other granite arches in Joshua Tree National Park, but none are as dramatic as this one.

After taking in the arch, head back on the stem trail to the loop. Go right/northeast onto it. The next branching trail is where you began the loop; go right/northeast onto the branching trail and retrace your steps back to the parking lot.

If staying at the campground, instead head from your campsite onto the 0.3-mile Arch Rock Trail to the loop. Go right/east onto the loop and take the next branching trail right/southeast to Arch Rock.

The entire trail is open to sunlight, so always don sunscreen, sunglasses and sunhat as well as carry plenty of water. Rattlesnakes and scorpions sometimes like to rest in rock crevices, so be careful where placing your hands if climbing on the rocks. Some rocks also can be too slippery for young children to climb, so exercise caution.

Other Trails to Arches

While Joshua Tree's arches can't match the size or number of those at Arches National Park, they are impressive nonetheless. Just consider that Arches' formations are carved out of soft sandstone while those at Joshua Tree were whittled out of hard granite. It's a testament to Mother Nature's patience... wind, rain, and the freeze-thaw cycle always win out.

Among the best arches and the trails to see them at Joshua Tree are:

• **Belle's Eye Arch** – An eye-shaped hole sits in a boulder about 0.6 miles (1.2-mile round trip) north of Belle Campground along the California Riding and Hiking Trail. The Moon Mat Cave also sits near the campground, off of Pinto Basin Road, in a two-for-one geology adventure.

• **Elephant Arch** – A series of rock formations that looks like an elephant features small arches to help give the "pachyderm" its shape. It sits in the southern portion of the Wonderland of Rocks rock climbing area north of Barker Dam and can be accessed, with some scrambling over and between boulders, from that trail.

- **Window Rock** – An arch that looks vaguely like a bird sits at the top of a rock wall along the Window Loop, a stacked loop off of the Maze Loop for a 5.3-mile hike. You'll also pass through fantastical rock formations, slot canyons, Joshua tree forests, and desert washes. The trailhead is off of Park Boulevard.

Desert Fauna
Cholla Cactus Garden Trail

Day hikers can walk through a forest of thousands of cholla cactus at the park.

The 0.25-mile Cholla Cactus Garden Trail loops through the otherworldly – and dangerous – sight. An excellent time to visit the garden is about an hour before sunset when the cacti seem to glow in the changing light. March through April also is a great time during the day, as the teddybear cholla are in bloom with their showy yellow- to white-colored flowers.

To reach the trailhead, from the park's Oasis Visitor Center on Utah Trail just south of Calif. Hwy. 62, take the former south. Once in the park, Utah Trail becomes Park Boulevard. Turn left/southeast onto Pinto Basin Road. About 12 miles from Park Boulevard, look for a parking lot on the road's south side. Park there.

The flat, hard-packed dirt trail leaves from the lot's southwest corner. Spreading for 10 acres around you is a desert landscape dominated by teddybear cholla.

It's a particularly unique site because creosote bush and burrobush rule the basin's expanse of alluvial fans. Few teddybear cholla can be found there.

This particular spot at the edge of the Colorado Desert, however, is ideal for teddybear cholla. About 4 inches of water seasonally flows out of Wilson Canyon over a loose mixture of broken rock and soil, which nicely holds the moisture. This spot in the Pinto Basin is for teddybear cholla what the Mediterranean is to humans.

The teddybear cholla, with its distinctive trunk, can grow up to 5 feet tall. A detachable sheath covers its sharp 1-inch needles.

Surprisingly, most of the cholla's seeds are infertile. Instead,

A 10-acre natural cholla cactus garden sits in Joshua Tree National Park's Pinto Basin. NPS photo.

it reproduces when stem joints fall off.

The stem joints easily detach from the parent plant. Thanks to tiny barbs on its spines, they quickly latch on to anything brushing against them – including you.

And as luck would have it, these barbs cause great pain when removed.

Because of this, do not wear open-toed sandals and stay on the trail...or stem joints will come home with you. Some cholla does reach out onto the trail, so keep an eye out for them and supervise children.

Sixteen markers also can be found along the trail. Pick up the brochure at the trailhead for the info on desert fauna that goes with each marker.

The trail is entirely open to the sun, so be sure to don sunscreen, sunglasses, and sunhat. Always carry extra water, even though this is a short trail.

Other Trails to Unique Desert Fauna

With several thousand feet of elevation change and the Mojave and Colorado deserts meeting in the park, an incredible variety of plants grow there. They range from the unique Joshua tree to the cholla cactus – each found in one desert rather than the other – to the ubiquitous scrub brush native to both desert floors while juniper and pinyon pine grow on mountainsides.

Among the best trails to see unique desert fauna at the park are:

• **Indian Cove Trail** – Day hikers can learn how Native Americans used various desert plants on this 0.6-mile loop at Indian Cove Campground's west end. The trail is a gently rolling path with a few built-in steps.

• **Panorama Loop** – Hikers can explore both a pinyon-juniper woodland and a dense Joshua tree forest as climbing 1100 feet over 6.6 miles from a sandy wash to a ridgeline on the Little San Bernardino Mountains. The trail leaves from the Black Rock Campground.

• **Willow Hole Trail** – The flat 7.2-mile out and back trail heads to an oasis of willow trees. Along the way, you'll travel through a Joshua tree forest, the Wonderland of Rocks boulders, and sandy washes. Start at the south terminal of the Boy Scout Trailhead off of Park Boulevard.

• **Pine City Trail** – A seasonal wash enclosed by large boulders crafted a cooler, moister microclimate than the surrounding desert, and it's perfect for pinyon pine. The trailhead of the 4.4-mile round trip hike is at the end of Desert Queen Mine Road.

Night Skies
Porcupine Wash-Ruby Lee Mill Site Trail

In most urban areas, artificial lighting and smog wash out the stars. Many people grow up only seeing a few of the brightest points in the night sky and never realizing the grandeur of the Milky Way that humankind has enjoyed for tens of thousands of years. But there still are places where one can seen an unpolluted night sky.

Among Southern California's darkest skies are those at Joshua Tree National Park. For many who've never seen the night sky before, the sight is absolutely startling and awe-inspiring.

Most campgrounds off the park's main roads offer great views, but the best place always is in the backcountry. One relatively remote yet easy to access spot for stargazing is the Porcupine Wash-Ruby Lee Mill Site Trail, located in the Pinto Basin.

The 8.8-mile loop is surrounded by the Hexie and Pinto mountains, which block the glow of nearby urban areas, and at night the nearby road is rarely traveled.

To reach the trailhead, from the Oasis Visitor Center on Utah Trail just south of Calif. Hwy. 62, take the former south. Once in the park, Utah Trail becomes Park Boulevard. Turn left/southeast onto Pinto Basin Road. In a little more than 16 miles, look for the Porcupine Wash trailhead parking lot on the road's eight/south side. Park in the lot.

You need not do the whole trail to enjoy the night sky. In fact, hiking the trail at night would be dangerous and require a flashlight that diminishes your ability to see the night sky.

Instead, arrive before sunset and simply hike a hundred or so yards in. Find a nice flat spot, sit back, and watch the stars suddenly appearing like pinpricks on the darkening sheet above.

Stars by the season

What you'll see in the night sky changes with each season.

In spring, two bright stars – orange Arcturus and blue Regulus – both are visible. The Big Dipper's handle points toward Arcturus, which appears near dusk in the eastern sky. To the south, Regulus is in the constellation Leo's front paw.

Summer brings the spectacular band of the Milky Way, which is best seen on a moonless night. The Summer Triangle features the three bright blue stars, Vega, Altair and Deneb. Mid-August marks the Perseid Meteor Shower. If visiting in summer, do not hike the trail during the day – it is dangerously hot – but nights are comfortable.

Autumn offers the Great Square of Pegasus, which rises in the northeastern sky at dusk. The Andromeda Galaxy is a fuzzy patch near the square. Autumn days are great for hiking the trail, but nights in the high desert can be cold.

Winter delivers the constellation Orion and the sky's brightest star, Sirius, which is only 8.6 light years from Earth. The red star Aldebaran is the winking eye in the constellation Taurus. While late winter can have pleasant days, nights will be very cold.

Stargazing pointers

Some quick tips for stargazing:

- **Go on moonless nights** – Reflecting sunlight to Earth, the moon can reduce the number of stars you'll see. Check the moon phases to find the perfect evening to stargaze.
- **Only use red lights** – The human eyes needs at least 20 minutes to adjust to low light. Bright non-red lights delay that process and can wash out the stars.
- **Layer your clothing** – The dry air at the higher elevations can make for chilly nights, even in summer. You'll probably

Best Sights to See at Joshua Tree NP

Joshua Tree National Park's dark skies, like those at Porcupine Wash, are the perfect spot to stargaze. NPS photo.

need a sweatshirt and jacket on July evenings, though during the day you would roast alive wearing that.

- **Watch your step** – Animals come out at night, and you don't want to accidently step on a snake...or into a cactus or on uneven rock. All will end your stargazing adventure.
- **Bring a folding chair** – One that you can lean back in will reduce neck strain. Sitting in one spot, even if you adjust the chair slightly to see different parts of the sky, will reduce the chances that you trample vegetation.
- **Carry water** – Many areas of the park, including Porcupine Wash, have no running water. Even if not hiking, the dry air will cause you to feel parched.

Hiking the trail

Should you decide to hike the trail during the day, spring is a great time to do so because of the many beautiful wildflowers. Birdwatching also is good there. There are plenty of jumbo rocks and boulders to explore and scrabble over. You won't find any Joshua trees here, though, as you're in the Colorado Desert, a subsection of the Sonoran Desert; Joshua trees only grow in the Mojave at higher elevations.

Go counterclockwise on the hike. You'll begin by passing a borrow pit. The northern part of the loop is a jeep trail and heads to the Ruby Lee Mill Site.

At the base of the Hexie Mountains, the trail curves south to begin the far side of the loop. It then joins the intermittent Porcupine Creek and follows the wash back to the borrow pit and parking lot.

The washes can be sandy, so be sure to wear hiking boots with good traction and to bring a trekking pole. A map and compass as well as plenty of water are a good idea. The entire trail is open to the sun, so be sure to don sunscreen, sunglasses and sunhat.

Desert Wildflowers
West Side Loop

Day hikers can spot a variety of wildflowers as exploring the washes and ridges of the park's northwest corner.

The 4.7-mile West Side Loop is easy to get to and offers a variety of experiences because of its 784-foot change in elevation. It doubles as an equestrian trail, so you'll definitely feel like you're in the Old West.

To reach the trailhead, from Calif. Hwy. 62 in Yucca Valley, go south on Joshua Lane. Turn right/west onto San Marino Drive, which upon curving south becomes Black Rock Canyon Road and enters the Black Rock Campground. Park at the Black Rock Nature Center.

Walk to the nature center's southwest corner and follow the blacktop road straight west. The trailhead is east of campsite #30.

In about 175 feet, the trail divides, beginning the loop. Go left/south to do the loop clockwise. The trail in short order joins Campground Road.

After passing a water tank, the trail at 0.2 miles splits from the road. The path quickly gains elevation, offering great views of the San Jacinto mountains to the southwest.

Several wildflowers can be seen along the trail, especially after wet winters, making El Niño years the best for viewing. When flowers bloom – and sometimes they don't bloom at all – varies annually, but usually they begin mid-February in Pinto Basin and at lower elevations. Most of the rest of the park, including this trail, sees blooms in March and April when temperatures warm. Elevations above 5000 feet can enjoy blooms as late as June.

At 0.3 miles, the loop junctions with Burnt Hill Trail. Continue right/southwest.

The vivid blue Canterbury bells like rocky slopes and washes like on this section of the trail. The fluted blossoms can stretch up to 1.5 inches long.

About a mile in, the trail joins a wash and disappears, as you begin the loop's southern side in Little Long Canyon. Turn right to follow the canyon west, as it continues to gain elevation. Stay right at a confluence; the wash will diminish and become a trail shortly thereafter.

As the trail winds through hills, look west for San Gorgonio Mountain. Southern California's tallest peak at 11,503 feet, on sunny winter and spring days its snowcap shines brilliantly.

About 1.7 miles in, the trail reaches its highest point at 4,510 feet. Pretty views of Warren Peak to the south and mountains beyond it await.

Continuing downhill, look for more desert wildflowers. Mojave aster often can be seen on the rocky hillsides at this elevation. The light purple flower with a bright yellow center can grow two inches wide.

At 2.3 miles, the trail enters a wash. You've reached the loop's southwest side. While losing the path is easy in a wash, you're on the right track if you pass a confluence at 2.6 miles.

Washes often are a favorite location for purple mat to grow. Tiny and colored like amethyst, they are close to the ground and to one another. From a distance, they appear like a single, violet rug.

At 3 miles, the trail leaves the wash, and it's uphill again (If while walking the wash you've come to a dirt road, you've gone too far and should backtrack.). The good news is the trail is fairly well-maintained and easy to follow from there.

You'll be delighted by the Joshua tree grove in the valley round you. Piñon trees thrive as well on the hillside.

The brilliant orange mariposa lily often can be seen in pin-

Several desert wildflowers, including the beavertail cactus, can be found across Joshua Tree National Park. NPS photo.

on-juniper woodlands. Not only their color but their height makes the flower stand out, as it grows atop stems between four to eight inches high. The blossom consists of three petals stretching a couple of inches apart.

At 3.15 miles, the trail turns east and begins the loop's northside. The trail then reaches its second peak at 3.6 miles in. While there are some ups and downs over rolling terrain, it's mainly downhill the rest of the way.

On the dry rocky slopes, watch for the magenta flower of the beavertail cactus. The blossom, which can be up to 3 inches wide, sits on the tip of the beavertail's flat, broad stems. This cactus can grow in clusters up to 6 feet wide, so when flowering they form a striking swath across the desert terrain.

The loop junctions with the Hi-View Nature Trail at 4 miles. A little farther along, the Hi-View – which is a side trail – rejoins the path. A popular vista because of its easy access and short length, you may want to consider taking the Hi-View if you have some extra energy to burn. It'll add 1.3 miles to the hike for a 6-mile route.

Desert globemallow likes the dry, rocky slopes such as those found around Hi-View. The orange, spherical blossom appears on shrubs that grow up to 3 feet high.

When wildflowers are in bloom, you're certain to see butterflies, a number of songbirds, and bees, of course. Other times of the year, rabbits and even a small deer or two can be spotted off trail.

At 4.7 miles (presuming you didn't go on the Hi-View), you'll arrive back at trailhead. Retrace your steps back to the Black Rock Nature Center, which is worth a stop just for the exhibits.

Be forewarned that there is virtually no shade on the trail, so always don sunscreen, sunglasses and sunhat, as well as bring plenty of drinking water. Hiking boots with good traction and a trekking pole will help you on the ascents and crossings of the sandy washes. A good topo map and compass are a must.

And don't forget a desert wildflower guidebook!

Other Trails to Desert Wildflowers

We often think of deserts as places of great desolation. The truth is plants abound there, and during spring after a wet winter or a good rainfall, millions of blooming wildflowers prove the point.

Unfortunately, the time to see wildflower blooms in the park is limited, with a couple of weeks sometime in March or April the narrow window. Check the national park's website for bloom updates.

Should you see a great flower bloom on the drive to or from the trailhead, don't walk into the flower bed, as doing so damages the fragile desert environment while increasing your chances of encountering rattlesnakes, which like to hide amid the blossoms.

Among the best trails to see wildflower booms at the park are:

- **Bajada Nature Trail** – The 0.25-mile loop heads over a bajada – a slope of alluvial material at the foot of a mountain – with a variety of Colorado Desert plants growing upon it. The trail is located south of Cottonwood Visitor Center off of Pinto Basin Road near the park's southern entry.
- **Barker Dam Trail** – Wildflowers along the 1.5-mile round trip include yellow fiddleneck, white woolly bluestar, red mistletoe berries, and beavertail cactus. The trailhead is off of Barker Dam Road, which branches from Park Boulevard.
- **Boy Scout Trail (southern trailhead)** – Another fantastic bloom to see in mid-April is the giant white blossoms of the Joshua tree. Each bloom is about the size of a pineapple and grows off the Joshua tree's arms. Between a half-dozen to 18 blossoms can be found on various Joshua trees. Pick up the trailhead on Park Boulevard.
- **Cap Rock Trail** – The 0.4-mile loop heads past desert wildflowers rising beneath Joshua trees as circling the fascinating Cap Rock formation. The Cap Rock parking area is at the junction of Park Boulevard and Keys View Road.
- **Fortynine Palms Oasis Trail** – Each spring, the ridge this 3-mile out and back trails hikes up and over lights up with the red-orange blooms of the barrel cactus. Access the trail from Forty-nine Palms Canyon Road off of Calif. Hwy. 62.
- **Indian Cove Trail** – Flowering yucca and various small

wildflowers can be seen on this short, 0.6-mile kid-friendly trail. The trailhead is off of Indian Cove Road West, which can be accessed from Hwy. 62.

- **Lost Horse Mine Trail** – A 4-mile round trip segment of this trail passes wildflowers on its way to an abandoned mine. Usually in mid-April a field of yellow flowers appears in Lost Horse Valley below; the flowers include golden linanthus, Wallace's woolly daisy, and bristly fiddlenecks. The trailhead is off of Lost Horse Mine Road, which branches off Keys View Road.
- **Maze Loop** – Though best known most for its granite jumbles, hikers also can see fields of Mojave Desert wildflowers, cactus gardens, and Joshua trees on this 6.5-miles route. The trailhead is off of Park Boulevard.
- **South Park Peak Trail** – Look for the lavender-petaled Mojave Aster on this 0.6-mile loop, which heads up to a peak overlooking Yucca Valley with great views of San Gorgonio Mountain and San Jacinto Peak. Technically not in the national park, it is accessed via the park's Black Rock Canyon Campground.
- **Split Rock Loop** – Most people hike this 2.5-mile loop to explore the Jumbo Rocks, but in spring the wildflowers steal the show. Among them are California indigo bush, cushion foxtail cactus, desert mariposa lily, desert paintbrush, false woolly daisy, Mojave sandwort, turpentine broom, and Wright's buckwheat. The trail starts at the Split Rock picnic area near Park Boulevard.
- **Willow Hole Trail** – Spring wildflowers usually are abundant on this 6.8-mile round trip trail that heads through a Joshua tree forest and alongside the Wonderland of Rocks. The trailhead is the Boy Scout Trail's southern end off of Park Boulevard.

Keys View offers a fantastic vista of the Coachella Valley at night. NPS photo.

Other Park Trails

Sometimes the best trails in a park are the ones few people know about. Those hikes don't always attract crowds because of their length, remoteness, or the feature there isn't usually associated with the park.

Such is the case with three trails at Joshua Tree National Park:

• **California Riding and Hiking Trail** – Though the trail runs 35 miles through the park, hikers can enjoy it in several short segments. One interesting section is a 1.25-mile stretch (2.5-mile round trip) heading from south/east from Ryan Campground through a canyon in an arm of the Little San Bernardino Mountains.

• **Crown Prince Lookout Trail** – During World War II, the military maintained an observation post for airplanes atop a granite formation. While the route is not maintained, the jeep trail that once led to the warning station still is visible. The

3.25-mile round trip hike leaves from Park Boulevard about a quarter mile west of the Jumbo Rocks Day Use parking lot and crosses a desert plateau en route to the outlook.

- **Keys View Trail** – The 0.25-mile paved loop path is short and steep but offers what probably are the park's most breathtaking views – the Coachella Valley, San Jacinto Peak, San Gorgonio Mountain, and the Salton Sea all can be seen from here. The trailhead is at the end of Keys View Road, which runs south from Park Boulevard.

Nearby Sights

While most think of Joshua Tree National Park as remote, it's actually quite close to several built-up areas – though a wide swath of preserved Mojave Desert does sit next it. Because of this, there are several nearby hiking areas that offer different experiences than what would be had at Joshua Tree. Anyone visiting the national park should consider taking some time to also check out these trails.

Big Morongo Canyon Preserve
Desert Willow Trail

When temperatures cool at Joshua Tree National Park, the best way for hikers to beat the chill is to lose a little elevation. A great spot to do that – especially in spring – is the Big Morongo Canyon Preserve, which is a couple of hundred feet lower.

Among the half-dozen trails to hike at the preserve, the Desert Willow Trail makes for a pleasant walk in which hikers can see flora more common to the Mojave than the Colorado desert, which the Coachella Valley sits in. The route runs about 1.3 miles when done in a loop with a couple of segments of the Marsh Trail.

To reach the trailhead, from Joshua Tree National Park take Calif. Hwy. 62 south to Morongo Valley. Turn left/south onto East Drive then left/southeast into the park. From the southeast side of the parking area, go on the stem trail.

At the first trail junction, turn left/northeast into the Marsh Trail. You'll cross a bridge. In about 200 feet from the parking lot kiosk, go left/north onto the dirt trail. You're now officially on the Desert Willow Trail.

Alkali goldenbush lines this section of the trail. The shrub grows up to 40 inches high and produces a brilliant yellow flower. It flourishes in arid, sandy soil, especially alkali flats, hence its name.

Clusters of wild desert rhubarb also grow along this part of the trail. The rhubarb's waxy and ridged leaves nicely capture moisture, even from mists, and sends it down a central vein to its taproot, in a sort of self-irrigation process. The plant grows about 2-4 feet tall and usually at a lower elevation than the preserve.

Stands of tall creosote bush also can be found here. A com-

A great spot to see desert plants – such as a blooming creosote – is the Big Morongo Canyon Preserve. BLM photo.

mon desert plant, creosote prefers the moist areas of washes and alluvial fans. Their roots are so efficient at absorbing water that they often prevent other desert plants from establishing themselves in an area. A creosote's crown also can split to create clones of itself; some colonies of the plant that grew from a single seed have been dated to 11,700 years old in California.

Another sight here is the desert willow, the trail's namesake. Despite the name, the shrub is not related to the weeping willow tree found across the United States. Still, the desert version found here can grow between 15-40 feet high.

In 0.4 miles and after crossing a bridge over an intermittent stream, the path junctions with the Yucca Ridge Trail. Go right/south.

As the trail runs along the base of Yucca Ridge with a desert wash to the trail's right, several stands of honey mesquite grow in dense thickets. The short tree serves as an important habitat for rabbits and quails.

Upon nearing the wetlands area, two observations decks – one on each side of the trail – let hikers enjoy the desert scenery stretching over the wash.

At 0.8 miles, the trail crosses the wetlands via bridge and junctions again with the Marsh Trail. Go right/west onto the Marsh Trail, a boardwalk.

The trail winds through the wetlands with a couple of large observation decks along the way. Among the interesting plants seen here is spikerush. It can grow close to seven feet high. As a grass, their stems usually can't support itself at that height, so they bend downward under their own weight and form a dense cover. It's the perfect shelter for small mammals and ground-nesting birds.

At 1.24 miles, the route reaches the junction with the Desert Willow Trail. Stay on the Marsh Trail by going left/southwest then take the next right/northwest onto the stem leading to the parking lot.

There's very little shade on the trail, so you'll want to don sunscreen, sunglasses and a sunhat for the hike. Dogs are not allowed in the preserve.

Marsh Trail

Day hikers can explore one of California's largest cottonwood and willow riparian areas only a few miles from Joshua Tree National Park.

The half-mile Marsh Trail at Big Morongo Canyon Preserve skirts then loops through the wetlands, a rare sight in the desert. An elevated boardwalk, the trail is wheelchair accessible.

To reach the preserve, from the national park, head south on

Though Joshua Tree National Park sits in the middle of the desert, a marsh can be hiked at nearby Big Morongo Canyon Preserve. BLM photo.

Calif. Hwy. 62, also known as the Twentynine Palms Highway. Go left/south on East Drive then left/east onto Covington Drive, which heads into the preserve and to a parking lot.

Begin the day hike on the access trail at the lot's southeast side. Upon reaching the first trail junction, go right/southwest. This is the trail's open desert section that passes the preserve's butterfly garden and education center.

At about 0.18 then at 0.2 miles, the boardwalk junctions with the looping Mesquite Trail. Veer left and stay on the boardwalk each time. The trail then curls north and enters the marsh.

The 31,000-acre preserve in the San Bernardino Mountains protects the riparian area and is overseen by the Bureau of Land Management. The preserve straddles the Mojave (the canyon's upper portion) and the Colorado (the lower section) deserts.

Water flows out of the surrounding mountains to form Big Morongo Creek, which cuts through a canyon created by the Morongo Fault. The water pools in the preserve's marsh, which attracts numerous birds, especially during the fall and spring migrations. Internationally recognized, more than 250 bird species have been spotted in the preserve with more than a quarter of them nesting on site.

Much of the boardwalk here is surrounded by thickets and shaded by the cottonwoods and willows, so the temperature is noticeably cooler than the desert portion of the hike. Several benches and decks to enjoy the birds and scenery can be found.

The birds flitting about here might surprise you. While there are the usual hawks and falcons, wrens and warblers, and hummingbirds and crows, keep an eye out for pelicans and an hear cocked for woodpeckers. Among the rarer of the latter is the gilded flicker, whose golden underwings can be seen when it flies.

Birds aren't the marsh's only denizens. After spring rains, wildflowers and butterflies alight the marsh with color. At dawn and dusk, if quiet, you often can glimpse other wildlife, including deer, bighorn sheep, raccoons and lizards, and predators like bobcats and coyotes.

At 0.36 miles from the trailhead is the first of two junctions with the Desert Willow Trail. Go left/northwest on the boardwalk, continuing through the marsh. In a few yards, you'll come to a large observation deck overlooking the marsh. After the trail curves to its western side, there's another broad deck.

The other junction with the Desert Willow Trail is just west of the second deck. Stay left and cross a bridge as you re-enter the desert. At the next junction, go right/northwest back to the parking lot.

San Gorgonio Mountain
Vivian Creek Trail

Hikers can ascend to the highest peak in Southern California from a trailhead that's just a short jaunt from Joshua Tree National Park.

Standing 11,503 feet high, San Gorgonio Mountain towers over all peaks in the Transverse Ranges and can be seen from a number of vantage points in the national park. It's a full 67 stories higher than San Jacinto Peak, the mountain that looms over nearby Palm Springs.

There are four main routes to reach the summit. The quickest of them is the Vivian Creek Trail, which will take about 10 hours. The hike comes to 18.5-miles round trip and gains 5,470 feet in elevation.

The length, steepness and high elevation makes it a difficult hike for most. You should first be able to summit San Jacinto Peak and Mt. Baldy (in the nearby San Gabriel Mountains) before even attempting this hike. You'll also need trekking poles and quality hiking boots to handle the terrain. Many hikers also recommend backpacking enough equipment – tent, sleeping bag, food and water – in case you get stranded a night or two on the mountain.

To reach the trailhead, from Joshua Tree National Park, take Calif. Hwy. 62 south to Interstate 10. Head west on the freeway across the San Gorgonio Pass. At exit 85, go left/northeast onto Oak Glen Road and drive through Yucaipa. Turn left/north onto Bryant Street then right/northeast onto Calif. Hwy. 38/Mill Creek Road. You'll soon enter the San Bernardino National Forest. Go right/east onto Valley of the Falls Drive. Take the road through Forest Falls to its end at the Vivian Creek Trailhead parking lot. This is about a 35-mile drive from where Hwy. 62 junctions with I-10.

Despite the hike's difficulty, the parking lot fills quickly on summer weekends. You'll want to arrive early, not just for a parking space but to ensure you're not hiking in the dark on your way back.

You'll also need a parking permit. A National Parks Pass (which includes entry into national forests), a Southern California Adventure Pass, or a day permit purchased at the ranger's office will work. Before setting out, always check the summit weather; conditions can change rapidly, so if you spot clouds forming at the peak any time after 10 a.m., turning back is smart.

A kiosk in the parking marks the way. At about 0.45 miles, look for a trail sign that sends you left and across the rock-strewn creek. Watch for a brown trail sign on the creek's other side so you re-enter the forest at the right spot.

From there, the trail narrows, turns rocky, and climbs for the next mile. The reward are great vistas of the neighboring peaks in the San Bernardino Mountains along the way.

At about 1.6 miles from the trailhead, the terrain flattens as you cross through an evergreen forest. Soon the trail heads alongside Vivian Creek, but the grade up is reasonable.

The trail reaches a junction at 3.3 miles. Go left and head toward High Creek. The other way goes to Halfway Creek. In short order, the trail climbs again on some switchbacks. They are a bit easier than the ascent made earlier in the hike, however, and the views only get better – among the sights is Mount Baldy, the highest point on the trail's right and close to 40 miles away as the crow flies.

Beware of altitude sickness at this point. You're well above a mile in altitude, and there really is less oxygen at higher altitudes. If you feel headache and nausea, take a rest and rehydrate yourself. If the headache and nausea return once you

A trail heads to the top of San Gorgonio Mountain, Southern California's highest point. USFS photo.

continue the hike, your safest bet is to turn back.

At around 5.8 miles is High Creek Camp, elev. 9,440 ft. The camp has water to refill your canteens and is a nice spot to take a break and enjoy a snack.

The trail continues to the summit by crossing a stream at High Creek and then up several switchbacks with rock eroded off the mountainside. San Gorgonio essentially is a massive block of quartz monzonite. As the Pacific and North American tectonic plates slide against one another, San Gorgonio's older rock is being thrust over younger rock below it on the mountain's north side.

The trail reaches a ridge at 7.3 miles. A short spur on the right heads to an observation point. The great vista of the terrain south of the mountain makes it another good place to rest.

Once you're feeling re-energized, continue on the main trail, which quickly starts gaining altitude. The terrain turns even rockier as the trees thin. Be sure to look to your right for some fantastic views of San Jacinto Peak, which towers over Palm Springs.

You'll spot your destination, San Gorgonio Mountain's peak, at about 7.5 miles. The trail also grows steep again as you head above the tree line and enter the barren, rock-filled region circling the summit. Look for cairns and signposts to guide you. You also may want to pull a jacket out of your backpack, as the open area gets quite windy, even on clear days.

The San Bernardino Peak Divide Trail junction is at 8.8 miles. Continue right. At the very next trail junction, go left and make the final ascent to the peak of what many call "Old Greyback."

San Gorgonio is Southern California's only peak with a significant portion of its slope above the tree line. Its peak is quite similar to that of Mt. Whitney, the highest mountain in California and the Lower 48. By the way, Mt. Whitney boasts the Lower 48's longest recorded line of sight between two peaks – it and San Gorgonio – at 190 miles.

A sign marks San Gorgonio summit. The 360 degrees view are incredible to say the least. You're also just high enough that you can make out the earth's curvature.

You will get chilled atop the peak. The average temperature here never gets higher than 50 degrees, and there's plenty of snow even in late May.

Once you've taken in the sights, retrace your steps back to the Vivian Creek trailhead.

San Jacinto Peak
San Jacinto Peak Trail

Towering 10,824 feet into the sky – a full 1.95 miles above Palm Springs – San Jacinto Peak is the highest point in the San Jacinto Mountains and Riverside County, and the sixth highest in the lower 48. Dominating the city's skyline, a former mayor once called it "Palm Springs' oceanfront."

And yes, you can hike to the peak.

A number of routes allow you to ascend the mountain, but the most popular and the easiest is the one – at 11.5 miles roundtrip with an elevation gain of 2400 feet – described here. The route actually consists of several connected trails, each with its own name.

The best way to tackle San Jacinto Peak is to cheat a little by taking the Palm Springs Aerial Tram. From Joshua Tree National Park, drive Calif. Hwy. 62 south to Interstate 10. Go west on the freeway. Take Exit 110, turn left/south to go under the freeway, and get back on it going east. Use the very next exit to get onto Calif. Hwy. 111 south and head to the tram's Valley Station, which sits at 2,634 feet elevation. The tram climbs 6000 feet and lets you start the hike at 8516 feet. There is a fee to use the tram.

The first thing you'll notice upon departing the tram is the refreshing scent of pines, which contrasts with the smokier creosote in the valley below. The next thing you'll realize – about a half-second later – is the cooler temperature. San Jacinto's summit can be 40 degrees colder than on the desert floor, and you're only two-thirds of the way there. Then, after taking a few steps, you'll probably wonder why you're breathing a lot harder. There really is less oxygen up there, so take it easy for a bit.

Fortunately, the tram's mountain station is a good spot to

acclimate yourself to the higher elevation. The station includes an observation area, restaurant, snack bar and gift shop.

From the station, walk into Mt. San Jacinto State Park by heading uphill and west to Round Valley. At the trail junction, go straight/west onto the Round Valley Trail to the Long Valley Ranger Station. Once there, fill out day use permit at ranger station box; this is important for rescuers in case you should get lost.

Just after the ranger station, or 0.25 miles from the tram station, the trail splits again. The Willow Creek Trail is to the south but go right/west into Round Valley.

The trail parallels an intermittent creek. You may spot coyote tracks in the sand or hear their yips and howls in the distance. They generally stick to themselves and so are no danger.

At the next junction, with the High Trail, you've reached the Round Valley Meadow at 9000 feet elevation. Go right/northwest, continuing on the Round Valley Trail.

The Cahuilla Indians called San Jacinto Peak *I a kitch* (or *Aya Kaich*), which translates to "smooth cliffs," an appropriate name given that the mountain's north escarpment at 10,000 feet is the most severe in all of North America. For the Cahuilla, this was the home of Dakush, their founder.

In 0.3 miles, the trail reaches a seasonal ranger station. There the Tamarack Valley Trail heads north as a spur to a campground just below Cornell Peak.

Euro-American settlers in the area began climbing San Jacinto Peak in the 1870s with the first recorded ascent in 1874. The Wheeler Survey followed in 1878 and officially named the mountain "San Jacinto Peak."

In that era, grizzly bears inhabited the mountain, but they've since disappeared from the region. More slowly disappearing is the survey's name for the peak, which increasingly is known as

San Jacinto Peak looms over Palm Springs and the Coachella Valley. CSP photo.

Mount San Jacinto.

A mile from the ranger station, at a little more than 9600 feet, the trail reaches Wellman Divide. Here it splits between the Wellman Cienega Trail going south and the San Jacinto Peak Trail going the opposite way. Turn right/north.

Lodgepole pines dominate at this higher elevation. Sporting twisted needles that spiral out, the highly adaptable lodgepole is among the few trees that can grow at a subalpine elevation. They depend upon forest fires to propagate, as heat breaks the pitch on their cones, releasing the seeds.

Upon leaving the pines, the trail makes a switchback through manzanita bushes. After completing the switchback, you'll probably notice a cool wind picking up and how taking a few steps is even more difficult than at the tram station. The good news is you're almost at the summit.

At 2.4 miles from Wellman Divide, go right/north onto the spur, also known as the Mt. San Jacinto Summit Trail. You'll pass an emergency stone shelter built by CCC in 1930s. For the last 300 yards, you'll scramble over granite boulders to the very top of San Jacinto Peak.

The views from the peak are fantastic. To the northwest is San Gorgonio Mountain, the highest summit in Southern California. Little San Bernardo Mountains rises in the northeast. Looking east, you can see Palm Springs and Cathedral City in the valley below. The Santa Rosa Mountains are to the southeast. And on the clearest of days, the gleaming blue of the Pacific Ocean is visible to the west. As naturalist John Muir wrote, "The view from San Jacinto is the most sublime spectacle to be found anywhere on this earth!"

After taking in the sights, retrace your steps back to the tram station.

The best time to hike the peak is during summer. Temperatures here will be a pleasant mid 70s while the desert floor bakes at 115 degrees. Also, bring plenty of water.

For more Palm Springs and Coachella Valley trails, see this title's companion book, **Day Hiking Trails of Palm Springs and the Coachella Valley**.

Amboy Crater
Amboy Crater Trail

Possibly one of the coolest hikes you can take in Southern California is this trek into the cinder cone of an extinct volcano. It's a long drive from any major city, but your kids will remember the hike forever.

Amboy Crater looms on the horizon in the Mojave Desert about an hour north of Joshua Tree National Park. Drivers on the old Route 66 can see the volcano from miles away, and before the coming of the freeway, many cross-country drivers would stop and hike it. A parking lot sits off of what used to be Route 66.

To reach the trailhead, from Joshua Tree National Park's Oasis Visitor Center, take Utah Trail north. In Twentynine Palms, turn right/east onto Amboy Road. The remote desert highway curves north between the Sheep Hole Mountains and Cleghorn Lakes Wilderness Area. At Amboy, turn left/west onto County Road 66, which is the old Route 66. A drive to Amboy Crater's parking lot is on the left/south.

The trek to Amboy Crater heads through a lava field that is about 6,000 years old. Some 24 square miles of lava flow – featuring lava lakes, spatter cones, basalt flows and collapsed lava tubes – surround the cinder cone.

The volcano's eruptions hurled huge boulders nearly a mile from the crater. Red-hot when they came out of the earth, today they're black, porous and lightweight.

Look down at the ground, and you might wonder if you're looking at a black and white photo of Mars. Interestingly, scientists are using Amboy Crater as an analog to better understand Martian volcanoes.

Amboy Crater hardly is devoid of life. In March, yellow wildflowers bloom across much of the lava field, finding niches in

6000-year-old Amboy Crater sits just off the famous Route 66 north of Joshua Tree National Park. Rob Bignell photo.

cracks between the basalt rocks and wherever wind had blown clay to cover the lava. Watch the sand, and you're certain to see tracks of various birds and lizards and possibly even that of a mountain lion.

The trail enters the cinder cone's west side through the breach, where lava broke through the cone as it formed thousands of years ago. At the top of the breach, trails lead into the cinder cone and up to the rim. The crater's diameter is 1,508 feet and a mile in circumference.

The crater actually is made of four cinder cones that erupted in successive explosions. The interior of the cinder cone contains lava dams. Ash and cinders formed the cone.

Steep trails head up to the rim. From there, the vast stretch of lava fields about the cinder cone crater is visible through the breach.

Don't try to head back to the trail by taking a shortcut down the cinder cone's sides. It's much too steep, with the scree is almost impossible to walk upon.

As the cone sits in the Mojave Desert, you'll need to bring extra water, no matter the season. March, September and October tend to offer the best days for hiking the crater.

When done with the hike, drive about three miles east to Roy's Motel Café for some refreshments. It's an iconic Route 66 stop. The motel/cafe/gas station and its sign in Amboy have been seen in a number of movies.

Bonus Section I: Day Hiking Primer

You'll get more out of a day hike if you research it and plan ahead. It's not enough to just pull over to the side of the road and hit a trail that you've never been on and have no idea where it goes. In fact, doing so invites disaster.

Instead, you should preselect a trail (This book's trail descriptions can help you do that). You'll also want to ensure that you have the proper clothing, equipment, navigational tools, first-aid kit, food and water. Knowing the rules of the trail and potential dangers along the way also are helpful. In this special section, we'll look at each of these topics to ensure you're fully prepared.

Selecting a Trail

For your first few hikes, stick to short, well-known trails where you're likely to encounter others. Once you get a feel for hiking, your abilities, and your interests, expand to longer and more remote trails.

Always check to see what the weather will be like on the trail you plan to hike. While an adult might be able to withstand wind and a sprinkle here or there, for kids it can be pure misery. Dry, pleasantly warm days with limited wind always are best when hiking with children.

Don't choose a trail that is any longer than the least fit person in your group can hike. Adults in good shape can go 8-

12 miles a day; for kids, it's much less. There's no magical number.

When planning the hike, try to find a trail with a mid-point payoff – that is something you and definitely any children will find exciting about half-way through the hike. This will help keep up everyone's energy and enthusiasm during the journey.

If you have children in your hiking party, consider a couple of additional points when selecting a trail.

Until children enter their late teens, they need to stick to trails rather than going off-trail hiking, which is known as bushwhacking. Children too easily can get lost when off trail. They also can easily get scratched and cut up or stumble across poisonous plants and dangerous animals.

Generally, kids will prefer a circular route to one that requires hiking back the way you came. The return trip often feels anti-climatic, but you can overcome that by mentioning features that all of you might want to take a closer look at.

Once you select a trail, it's time to plan for your day hike. Doing so will save you a lot of grief – and potentially prevent an emergency. You are, after all, entering the wilds, a place where help may not be readily available.

When planning your hike, follow these steps:

• Print a road map showing how to reach the parking lot near the trailhead. Outline the route with a transparent yellow highlighter and write out the directions.

• Print a satellite photo of the parking area and the trailhead. Mark the trailhead on the photo.

• Print a topo map of the trail. Outline the trail with the yellow highlighter. Note interesting features you want to see along the trail and the destination.

• If carrying GPS, program this information into your device.

• Make a timeline for your trip, listing: when you will leave home; when you will arrive at the trailhead; your turn back time; when you will return for home in your vehicle; and when you will arrive at your home.

- Estimate how much water and food you will need to bring based on the amount of time you plan to spend on the trail and in your vehicle. You'll need at least two pints of water per person for every hour on the trail.
- Fill out two copies of a hiker's safety form. Leave one in your vehicle.
- Share all of this information with a responsible person remaining in civilization, leaving a hiker's safety form with them. If they do not hear from you within an hour of when you plan to leave the trail in your vehicle, they should contact authorities to report you as possibly lost.

Clothing

Footwear

If your feet hurt, the hike is over, so getting the right footwear is worth the time. Making sure the footwear fits before hitting the trail also is a good idea. With children, if you've gone a few weeks without hiking, that's plenty of time for feet to grow, and they may have just outgrown their hiking boots. Check out everyone's footwear a few days before heading out on the hike. If it doesn't fit, replace it.

For flat, smooth, dry trails, sneakers and cross-trainers are fine, but if you really want to head onto less traveled roads or tackle areas that aren't typically dry, you'll need hiking boots. Once you start doing any rocky or steep trails – and remember that a trail you consider moderately steep needs to be only half that angle for a child to consider it extremely steep – you'll want hiking boots, which offer rugged tread perfect for handling rough trails.

Socks

Socks serve two purposes: to wick sweat away from skin and to provide cushioning. Cotton socks aren't very good for hiking, except in extremely dry environments, because they retain moisture that can lead to blisters. Wool socks or liner socks work best. You'll want to look for three-season socks, also known as trekking socks. While a little thicker than summer socks, their extra cushioning generally prevents blisters. Also, make sure kids don't put on holey socks; that's just inviting blisters.

Layering

On all but hot, dry days, when hiking you should wear multiple layers of clothing that provide various levels of protection against sweat, heat loss, wind and potentially rain. Layering works because the type of clothing you select for each stratum serves a different function, such as wicking moisture or shielding against wind. In addition, trapped air between each layer of clothing is warmed by your body heat. Layers also can be added or taken off as needed.

Generally, you need three layers. Closest to your skin is the wicking layer, which pulls perspiration away from the body and into the next layer, where it evaporates. Exertion from walking means you will sweat and generate heat, even if the weather is cold. The second layer provides insulation, which helps keep you warm. The last layer is a water-resistant shell that protects you from rain, wind, snow and sleet.

As the seasons and weather change, so does the type of clothing you select for each layer. The first layer ought to be a loose-fitting T-shirt in summer, but in winter and on other cold days you might opt for a long-sleeved moisture-wicking synthetic material, like polypropylene. During winter, the next layer probably also should cover the neck, which often is exposed to the elements. A turtleneck works fine, but preferably not one made of cotton. The third layer in winter, depending on the temperature, could be a wool sweater, a half-zippered long sleeved fleece jacket, or a fleece vest.

You might even add a fourth layer of a hooded parka with pockets, made of material that can block wind and resist water. Gloves or mittens as well as a hat also are necessary on cold days.

Headgear

Half of all body heat is lost through the head, hence the hiker's adage, "If your hands are cold, wear a hat." In cool, wet weather, wearing a hat is at least good for avoiding hypothermia, a potentially deadly condition in which heat loss occurs faster than the body can generate it. Children are more susceptible to hypothermia than adults.

Especially during summer, a hat with a wide brim is useful in keeping the sun out of eyes. It's also nice should rain start falling.

For young children, get a hat with a chin strap. They like to play with their hats, which will fly off in a wind gust if not fastened some way to the child.

Sunglasses

Sunglasses are an absolute must if walking through open areas exposed to the sun and in winter when you can suffer from snow blindness. Look for 100% UV-protective shades, which provide the best screen.

Equipment

A couple of principles should guide your purchases. First,

the longer and more complex the hike, the more equipment you'll need. Secondly, your general goal is to go light. Since you're on a day hike, the amount of gear you'll need is a fraction of what backpackers shown in magazines and catalogues usually carry. Still, the inclination of most day hikers is to not carry enough equipment. For the lightness issue, most gear today is made with titanium and siliconized nylon, ensuring it is sturdy yet fairly light. While the following list of what you need may look long, it won't weigh much.

Backpacks

Sometimes called daypacks (for day hikes or for kids), backpacks are essential to carry all of the essentials you need – snacks, first-aid kit, extra clothing.

For day hiking, you'll want to get an internal frame, in which the frame giving the backpack its shape is inside the pack's fabric so it's not exposed to nature. Such frames usually are lightweight and comfortable. External frames have the frame outside the pack, so they are exposed to the elements. They are excellent for long hikes into the backcountry when you must carry heavy loads.

As kids get older, and especially after they've been hiking for a couple of years, they'll want a "real" backpack. Unfortunately, most backpacks for kids are overbuilt and too heavy. Even light ones that safely can hold up to 50 pounds are inane for most children.

When buying a daypack for your child, look for sternum straps, which help keep the strap on the shoulders. This is vital for prepubescent children, as they do not have the broad shoulders that come with adolescence, meaning packs likely will slip off and onto their arms, making them uncomfortable and difficult to carry. Don't buy a backpack that a child will "grow into." Backpacks that don't fit well simply will lead to sore shoulder and back muscles and could result in poor posture.

Also, consider purchasing a daypack with a hydration system for kids. This will help ensure they drink a lot of water. More on this later when we get to canteens.

Before hitting the trail, always check your children's backpacks to make sure that they have not overloaded them. Kids think they need more than they really do. They also tend to overestimate their own ability to carry stuff. Sibling rivalries often lead to children packing more than they should in their rucksacks, too. Don't let them overpack "to teach them a lesson," though, as it can damage bones and turn the hike into a bad experience.

A good rule of thumb is no more than 25 percent capacity. Most upper elementary school kids can carry only about 10 pounds for any short distance. Subtract the weight of the backpack, and that means only 4-5 pounds in the backpack. Overweight children will need to carry a little less than this or they'll quickly be out of breath.

Child carriers

You'll have to carry infant and toddlers. Until infants can hold their heads up, which usually doesn't happen until about four to six months of age, a front pack (like a Snugli or Baby Bjorn) is best. It keeps the infant close for warmth and balances out your backpack. At the same time, though, you must watch for baby overheating in a front pack, so you'll need to remove the infant from your body at rest stops.

Once children reach about 20 pounds, they typically can hold their heads up and sit on their own. At that point, you'll want a baby carrier (sometimes called a child carrier or baby backpack), which can transfer the infant's weight to your hips when you walk. You'll not only be comfortable, but your child will love it, too.

Look for a baby carrier that is sturdy yet lightweight. Your child is going to get heavier as time passes, so about the only way you can counteract this is to reduce the weight of the items you use to carry things. The carrier also should have adjustment points, as you don't want your child to outgrow the carrier too soon. A padded waist belt and padded shoulder straps are necessary for your comfort. The carrier should provide some kind of head and neck support if you're hauling an infant. It also should offer back support for children of all ages, and leg holes should be wide enough so there's no chafing. You want to be able to load your infant without help, so it should be stable enough to stand that way when you take it off the child can sit in it for a moment while you get turned around. Stay away from baby carriers with only shoulder straps, as you need the waist belt to help shift the child's weight to your hips for more comfortable walking.

Fanny packs

Also known as a belt bag, a fanny pack is virtually a must for anyone with a baby carrier, as you can't otherwise lug a backpack. If your significant other is with you, he or she can carry the backpack, of course. Still, the fanny pack also is a good alternative to a backpack in hot weather, as it will reduce back sweat.

If you have only one or two kids on a hike, or if they also are old enough to carry daypacks, your fanny pack need not be large. A mid-size pouch can carry at least 200 cubic inches of supplies, which is more than enough to accommodate all the materials you need. A good fanny pack also has a spot for hooking canteens to.

Canteens

Canteens or plastic bottles filled with water are vital for any hike, no matter how short the trail. You'll need to have enough of them to carry about two pints of water per person for every hour of hiking.

Trekking poles

Also known as walking poles or walking sticks, trekking poles are necessary for maintaining stability on uneven or wet surfaces and to help reduce fatigue. The latter makes them useful on even surfaces. By transferring weight to the arms, a trekking pole can reduce stress on your knees and lower back, allowing you to maintain a better posture and to go farther.

If an adult with a baby or toddler on your back, you'll primarily want a trekking pole to help you maintain your balance, even if on a flat surface, and to help absorb some of the impact of your step.

Graphite tips provide the best traction. A basket just above the tip is a good idea so the stick doesn't sink into mud or sand. Angled cork handles are ergonomic and help absorb sweat from your hands so they don't blister. A strap on the handle to wrap around your hand is useful so the stick doesn't slip out. Telescopic poles are a good idea as you can adjust them as needed based on the terrain you're hiking and as kids grow to accommodate their height.

The pole also needs to be sturdy enough to handle rugged terrain, as you don't want a pole that bends when you press it to the ground. Spring-loaded shock absorbers help when heading down a steep incline but aren't necessary. Indeed, for a short walk across flat terrain, the right length stick is about all you need.

Carabiners

Carabiners are metal loops, vaguely shaped like a D, with a sprung or screwed gate. You'll find that hooking a couple of them to your backpack or fanny pack useful in many ways. For example, if you need to dig through a fanny pack, you can hook the strap of your trekking pole to it. Your hat, camera straps, first-aid kit, and a number of other objects also can connect to them. Hook carabiners to your fanny pack or backpack upon purchasing them so you don't forget them when packing. Small carabiners with sprung gates are inexpensive, but they do have a limited life span of a couple of dozen hikes.

Navigational Tools
Paper maps

Paper maps may sound passé in this age of GPS, but you'll find the variety and breadth of view they offer to be useful. During the planning process, a paper map (even if viewing it online), will be far superior to a GPS device. On the hike, you'll also want a backup to GPS. Or like many casual hikers, you may not own GPS at all, which makes paper maps indispensable.

Standard road maps (which includes printed guides and handmade trail maps) show highways and locations of cities and parks. Maps included in guidebooks, printed guides handed out at parks, and those that are hand-drawn tend to be designed like road maps, and often carry the same positives and negatives.

Topographical maps give contour lines and other important details for crossing a landscape. You'll find them invaluable on a hike into the wilds. The contour lines' shape and their spacing on a topo map show the form and steepness of a hill or bluff, unlike the standard road map and most brochures and hand-drawn trail maps. You'll also know if you're in a woods, which is marked in green, or in a clearing, which is marked in white. If you get lost, figuring out where you are and how to get to where you need to be will be much easier with such information.

Aerial photos offer a view from above that is rendered exactly as it would look from an airplane. Thanks to Google and other online services, you can get fairly detailed pictures of the landscape. Such pictures are an excellent resource when researching a hiking trail. Unfortunately, those pictures don't label what a feature is or what it's called, as would a topo map. Unless there's a stream, determining if a feature is a valley bottom or a ridgeline also can be difficult. Like topo maps, satellite and aerial photos can be out of date a few years.

GPS

By using satellites, the global positioning system can find your spot on the Earth to within 10 feet. With a GPS device, you can preprogram the trailhead location and mark key turns and landmarks as well as the hike's end point. This mobile map is a powerful technological tool that almost certainly ensures you won't get lost – so long as you've correctly programmed the information. GPS also can calculate travel time and act as a compass, a barometer and altimeter, making such devices vir-tually obsolete on a hike.

In remote areas, however, reception is spotty at best for GPS, rendering your mobile map worthless. A GPS device also runs on batteries, and there's always a chance they will go dead. Or you may drop your device, breaking it in the process. Their screens are small, and sometimes you need a large paper map to get a good sense of the natural landmarks around you.

Compass

Like a paper map, a compass is indispensable even if you use GPS. Should your GPS no longer function, the compass then can be used to tell you which direction you're heading. A protractor compass is best for hiking. Beneath the compass needle is a transparent base with lines to help your orient yourself. The compass often serves as a magnifying glass to help you make out map details. Most protractor compasses also come with a lanyard for easy carrying.

Food and Water

Water

As water is the heaviest item you'll probably carry, there is a temptation to not take as much as one should. Don't skimp on the amount of water you bring, though; after all, it's the one supply your body most needs. It's always better to end up having more water than needed than returning to your vehicle dehydrated.

How much water should you take? Adults need at least a quart for every two hours hiking. Children need to drink about a quart every two hours of walking and more if the weather is hot or dry. To keep kids hydrated, have them drink at every rest stop.

Don't presume there will be drinking water on the hiking trail. Most trails outside of urban areas lack such an amenity. In addition, don't drink water from local streams, lakes, rivers or ponds. There's no way to tell if local water is safe or not. As soon as you have consumed half of your water supply, you should turn around for the vehicle.

Food

Among the many wonderful things about hiking is that

snacking between meals isn't frowned upon. Unless going on an all-day hike in which you'll picnic along the way, you want to keep everyone in your hiking party fed, especially as hunger can lead to lethargic and discontented children. It'll also keep young kids from snacking on the local flora or dirt. Before hitting the trail, you'll want to repackage as much of the food as possible as products sold at grocery stores tend to come in bulky packages that take up space and add a little weight to your backpack. Place the food in re-sealable plastic bags.

Bring a variety of small snacks for rest stops. You don't want kids filling up on snacks, but you do need them to maintain their energy levels if they're walking or to ensure they don't turn fussy if riding in a child carrier. Go for complex carbohydrates and proteins for maintaining energy. Good options include dried fruits, jerky, nuts, peanut butter, prepared energy bars, candy bars with a high protein content (nuts, peanut butter), crackers, raisins and trail mix (called "gorp"). A number of trail mix recipes are available online; you and your children may want to try them out at home to see which ones you collectively like most.

Salty treats rehydrate better than sweet treats do. Chocolate and other sweets are fine if they're not all that's served, but remember they also tend to lead to thirst and to make sticky messes. Whichever snacks you choose, don't experiment with food on the trail. Bring what you know kids will like.

Give the first snack within a half-hour of leaving the trailhead or you risk children becoming tired and whiny from low energy levels. If kids start asking for them every few steps even after having something to eat at the last rest stop, consider timing snacks to reaching a seeable landmark, such as, "We'll get out the trail mix when we reach that bend up ahead."

Milk for infants

If you have an infant or unweaned toddler with you, milk is as necessary as water. Children who only drink breastfed milk but don't have their mother on the hike require that you have breast-pumped milk in an insulated beverage container (such as a Thermos) that can keep it cool to avoid spoiling. Know how much the child drinks and at what frequency so you can bring enough. You'll also need to carry the child's bottle and feeding nipples. Bring enough extra water in your canteen so you can wash out the bottle after each feeding. A handkerchief can be used to dry bottles between feedings.

Don't forget the baby's pacifier. Make sure it has a string and hook attached so it connects to the baby's outfit and isn't lost.

What not to bring

Avoid soda and other caffeinated beverages, alcohol, and energy pills. The caffeine will dehydrate children as well as you. Alcohol has no place on the trail; you need your full faculties when making decisions and driving home. Energy pills essentially are a stimulant and like alcohol can lead to bad calls. If you're tired, get some sleep and hit the trail another day.

First-aid Kit

After water, this is the most essential item you can carry.

A first-aid kit should include:
- Adhesive bandages of various types and sizes, especially butterfly bandages (for younger kids, make sure they're colorful kid bandages)
- Aloe vera
- Anesthetic (such as Benzocaine)
- Antacid (tablets)

- Antibacterial (aka antibiotic) ointment (such as Neosporin or Bacitracin)
- Anti-diarrheal tablets (for adults only, as giving this to a child is controversial)
- Anti-itch cream or calamine lotion
- Antiseptics (such as hydrogen peroxide, iodine or Betadine, Mercuroclear, rubbing alcohol)
- Baking soda
- Breakable (or instant) ice packs
- Cotton swabs
- Disposable syringe (w/o needle)
- Epipen (if children or adults have allergies)
- Fingernail clippers (your multi-purpose tool might have this, and if so you can dispense with it)
- Gauze bandage
- Gauze compress pads (2x2 individually wrapped pad)
- Hand sanitizer (use this in place of soap)
- Liquid antihistamine (not Benadryl tablets, however, as children should take liquid not pills; be aware that liquid antihistamines may cause drowsiness)
- Medical tape
- Moisturizer containing an anti-inflammatory
- Mole skin
- Pain reliever (aka aspirin; for children's pain relief, use liquid acetaminophen such Tylenol or liquid ibuprofen; never give aspirin to a child under 12)
- Poison ivy cream (for treatment)
- Poison ivy soap
- Powdered sports drinks mix or electrolyte additives
- Sling
- Snakebite kit
- Thermometer

- Tweezers (your multi-purpose tool may have this allowing you to dispense with it)
- Water purification tablets

If infants are with you, be sure to also carry teething ointment (such as Orajel) and diaper rash treatment.

Many of the items should be taken out of their store packaging to make placement in your fanny pack or backpack easier. In addition, small amounts of some items – such as baking soda and cotton swabs – can be placed inside re-sealable plastic bags, since you won't need the whole amount purchased.

Make sure the first-aid items are in a waterproof container. A re-sealable plastic zipper bag is perfectly fine. If hiking in a humid or wet climate, be sure to replace the adhesive bandages every couple of months, as they can deteriorate in the moistness. Also, check your first-aid kit every few trips and after any hike in which you've just used it, so that you can replace used components and to make sure medicines haven't expired.

If you have older elementary-age kids and teenagers who've been trained in first aid, giving them a kit to carry as well as yourself is a good idea. Should they find themselves lost or if you cannot get to them for a few moments, the kids might need to provide very basic first aid to one another.

Hiking with Children: Attitude Adjustment

To enjoy hiking with kids, you'll first have to adopt your child's perspective. Simply put, we must learn to hike on our kids' schedules – even though they may not know that's what we're doing.

Compared to adults, kids can't walk as far, they can't walk as fast, and they will grow bored more quickly. Every step we take requires three for them. In addition, early walkers, up to two years of age, prefer to wander than to "hike." Preschool kids will start to walk the trail, but at a rate of only about a mile per hour. With stops, that can turn a three-mile hike into a four-hour journey. Kids also won't be able to hike as steep of trails as you or handle as inclement of weather as you might.

This all may sound limiting, especially to long-time backpackers used to racking up miles or bagging peaks on their hikes, but it's really not. While you may have to put off some backcountry and mountain climbing trips for a while, it also opens to you a number of great short trails and nature hikes with spectacular sights that you may have otherwise skipped because they weren't challenging enough.

So sure, you'll have to make some compromises, but the payout is high. You're not personally on the hike to get a workout but to spend quality time with your children.

Family Dog

Dogs are part of the family, and if you have children, they'll want to share the hiking experience with their pets. In turn, dogs will have a blast on the trail, some larger dogs can be used as Sherpas, and others will defend against threatening animals.

But there is a downside to dogs. Many will chase animals and so run the risk of getting lost or injured. Also, a doggy bag will have to be carried for dog pooh – yeah, it's natural, but also inconsiderate to leave for other hikers to smell and for their kids to step in. In addition, most dogs almost always will lose a battle against a threatening animal, so there's a price to be paid for your safety.

Many places where you'll hike solve the dilemma for you as dogs aren't allowed on their trails. Dogs are verboten on some state and national parks trails but usually permitted on those in national forests. Always check with the park ranger before heading to the trail.

If you can bring a dog, make sure it is well behaved and friendly to others. You don't need your dog biting another hiker while unnecessarily defending the family.

Rules of the Trail

Ah, the woods or a wide open meadow, peaceful and quiet, not a single soul around for miles. Now you and your children can do whatever you want.

Not so fast.

Act like wild animals on a hike, and you'll destroy the very aspects of the wilds that make them so attractive. You're also likely to end up back in civilization, specifically an emergency room. And there are other people around. Just as you would wish them to treat you courteously, so you and your children should do the same for them.

Let's cover how to act civilized on the trail.

Minimize damage to your surroundings

When on the trail, follow the maxim of "Leave no trace." Obviously, you shouldn't toss litter on the ground, start rockslides, or pollute water supplies. How much is damage and how much is good-natured exploring is a gray area, of course. Most serious backpackers will say you should never pick up objects, break branches, throw rocks, pick flowers, and so on – the idea is not to disturb the environment at all.

Good luck getting a four-year-old to think like that. The good news is a four-year-old won't be able to throw around many rocks or break most branches.

Still, children from their first hike into the wilderness should be taught to respect nature and to not destroy their environment. While you might overlook a preschooler hurling rocks into a puddle, they can be taught to sniff rather than pick flowers. As they grow older, you can teach them the value of leaving the rock alone. Regardless of age, don't allow children to write on boulders or carve into trees.

Many hikers split over picking berries. To strictly abide by the "minimize damage" principle, you wouldn't pick any berries at all. Kids, however, are likely to find great pleasure in eating blackberries, currants and thimbleberries as ambling down the trail. Personally, I don't see any problem enjoying a few berries if the long-term payoff is a respect and love for nature. To minimize damage, teach them to only pick berries they can reach from the trail so they don't trample plants or deplete food supplies for animals. They also should only pick what they'll eat.

Collecting is another issue. In national and most state and county parks, taking rocks, flower blossoms and even pine cones is illegal. Picking flowers moves many species, especially if they are rare and native, one step closer to extinction. Archeological ruins are extremely fragile, and even touching them can damage a site.

But on many trails, especially gem trails, collecting is part of the adventure. Use common sense – if the point of the trail is to find materials to collect, such as a gem trail, take judiciously, meaning don't overcollect. Otherwise, leave it there.

Sometimes the trail crosses private land. If so, walking around fields, not through them, always is best or you could damage a farmer's crops.

Pack out what you pack in

Set the example as a parent: Don't litter yourself; whenever stopping, pick up whatever you've dropped; and always require kids to pick up after themselves when they litter. In the spirit of "Leave no trace," try to leave the trail cleaner than you found it, so if you come across litter that's safe to pick up, do so and bring it back to a trash bin in civilization. Given this, you may want to bring a plastic bag to carry out garbage.

Picking up litter doesn't just mean gum and candy wrappers but also some organic materials that take a long time to decompose and aren't likely to be part of the natural environment you're hiking. In particular, these include peanut shells, orange peelings, and eggshells.

Burying litter, by the way, isn't viable. Either animals or erosion soon will dig it up, leaving it scattered around the trail and woods.

Stay on the trail
Hiking off trail means potentially damaging fragile growth. Following this rule not only ensures you minimize damage but is also a matter of safety. Off trail is where kids most likely will encounter dangerous animals and poisonous plants. Not being able to see where they're stepping also increases the likelihood of falling and injuring themselves. Leaving the trail raises the chances of getting lost. Staying on the trail also means staying out of caves, mines or abandoned structures you may encounter. They are usually dangerous places.

Finally, never let children take a shortcut on a switchback trail. Besides putting them on steep ground upon which they could slip, their impatient act causes the switchback to erode.

Trail Dangers

While hikers generally are safe from animals on Joshua Tree National Park trails, sometimes a misstep or poor decision can lead to problems.

Mountian lions

North America's largest cat roams the mountain ranges surrounding the national park and sometimes will come down to the desert floor in search of a meal. But the cats are rarely seen, like to keep to themselves, and typically are only active dusk through dawn.

Usually mountain lions, also known as cougars, don't want to be seen and will remain hidden, but there are stories of hungry lions that have attacked hikers.

Watch for signs of mountain lions, like paw prints, droppings, claw marks on trees, or the smell of carrion. If you see any of these indications, turn back.

If you encounter a mountain lion, don't turn your back to it but keep your space and give it time to retreat. If traveling in a group, gather everyone into a single cluster and get noisy. If the mountain lion approaches, wave you trekking poles and shout. You want to appear big to intimidate it, so don't crouch, bend over or down to pick up children, or run. All of those moves make you look smaller. If children are about to panic and run, though, then it's usually smarter to grab them.

Should a mountain lion attack, fight back in any way you can. Remember that the lion almost certainly will be stronger and faster than you. Try to protect your neck and head.

Snakes

Rattlesnakes live in the national park, but fortunately they are most active from April through October when the heat keeps hikers off the trail. In addition, poisonous snakes don't always inject venom when they bite, and some only spew a small amount that is survivable.

You can avoid snakes by staying out of desert scrub. Don't stick hands into dark holes and rocky crevices, don't turn over rocks, and don't hike at dusk or night when many snakes hunt. While climbing rocks, be careful where you stick your hand as a snake may be sunning itself.

If you see a snake, slowly back away from it. If you hear a rattle, stand still. In both cases, the snake usually will scoot off. Don't try to get a closer look, as it invites attack, especially from a rattler, because it then feels cornered. A snake can strike at about a third of its body length, so you'll probably be just far enough away that it won't strike. Also, don't mess with baby snakes for they too will bite.

Sometimes hikers walking through desert scrub don't even realize they've been bitten (this is why staying on the clear trail is vital), and sometimes you stumble a little too close to a snake. Bite symptoms include pain and burning at the bite site followed by swelling and blistering. Nausea and vomiting, with numbness and tingling about the mouth, fingers and scalp also are indications. If the bite is severe, the victim also will grow faint and dizzy and have a weak pulse and cold, clammy skin. They may go into shock.

To treat a snake bite, lay down and control your panic. Place a compression bandage lightly above the bite, as this can slow the spread of venom. Do not use a tourniquet, however. Then call for help and seek medical attention immediately.

Finally, if at all possible try to identify the snake so the right anti-venom can be used when the victim receives medical treatment.

Scorpions

Scorpions native to Joshua Tree National Park generally are on the weak side where venom is concerned, and their sting often doesn't hurt more than a bee's. However, the nonnative bark scorpion – the most venomous of America's scorpions –

have been spotted in nearby Indio, Calif., since 2015.

You can avoid a scorpion sting by keeping your hands out of holes and crevices as well as by not overturning rocks, all of which could be homes for these little arthropods.

If stung, you'll feel instant pain or burning, numbness and tingling, and the bitten area will be sensitive to touch.

Treatment includes washing the stung area with soap and water then applying a cold compress to it. You also should elevate a stung limb above heart level. Always bring a young child stung by a scorpion to the emergency room. For older teens, if reactions in addition to those previously listed appear, bring them as well to the ER.

Spiders

Most spider bites are harmless, but the national park's black widow is an exception.

Unfortunately, most hikers don't know they've even been bit, as it feels like a pinprick. As with mosquitoes, the reaction to a spider bite is mostly just a nuisance. Still, allergic reactions can occur, and a few spiders are downright deadly.

If you feel an immediate burning, pain, redness and swelling, especially around a double fang mark, you probably are the victim of a black widow and should seek immediate medical attention.

To avoid spider bites, don't stick hands into dark holes or rocky crevices and don't turn over rocks. Spiders live in such areas and may bite if surprised and think they're under attack.

Treat a spider bite by washing the bite area with soap and water. A cold compress can help alleviate the swelling and redness. Diphenhydramine tablets can be taken to reduce the itch while acetaminophen will help relieve severe pain. If a severe reaction occurs or you know the bite was from a poisonous spider, seek immediate medical treatment.

A few don'ts ... Aspirin won't reduce the inflammation of a spider bite and shouldn't be taken by children. Don't bother with antibiotics, as they're not designed for treating spider bites. Finally, don't cut open the bite mark, as it may lead to infection.

Ants

The nonnative fire ant can now be found in the national park. Usually they attack en masse when a hiker inadvertently steps on their mound. Their stings can send you into anaphylaxis, a life-threatening allergic reaction to the venom that can lead to a coma or death.

Avoid ants of any type by being careful not to toss your gear on an ant hill or by sitting against a tree with sap, which ants may feed upon. They typically come out after a heavy rain.

While all of these dangers are real, fortunately animal attacks on hikers are extremely rare. Far, far greater dangers to any hiker are dehydration, heat stroke and sun stroke. See the introduction for tips on avoiding these medical emergencies.

For more about these topics and many others, pick up this author's **Hikes with Tykes: A Practical Guide to Day Hiking with Kids**. You also can find tips online at the author's **Day Hiking Trails** blog (*hikeswithtykes.blogspot.com*). Have fun on the trail!

Bonus Section II: National Parks Primer

The breadth of wonders at America's national parks astounds the mind. You can stand at the nation's rooftop with 60 peaks taller than 12,000 feet at Rocky Mountain National Park or in a gash in the earth more than a mile deep at Grand Canyon. You can visit among the driest places in the world where little more than an inch of rain falls per year upon the beige sands of Death Valley or step into the blue ocean itself at Biscayne National Park where the bulk of the wilderness is the Atlantic and its vibrantly colored coral reefs. You can see some of the oldest rock on Earth, like the 1.2 billion year-old granite at Shenandoah National Park, to some of the newest land on the planet at Hawai'i Volcanoes National Park where lava flows create new ground inch by inch be-fore you. You can enjoy parks that are primarily historical and even urban in nature, such as Cuyahoga Valley National Park, which features pioneer farms and bicycle paths, while others preserve breathless, awe-inspiring tracts of wilderness and stone, such as Yosemite's El Capitan and Half Dome. You can trek through caves with rooms larger than a football field hundreds of feet below the ground, such as at Carlsbad Cav-erns, or beneath trees soaring 15 stories over your head at Redwood National Park.

Given these grand wonders, not surprisingly national parks are a major travel destination. Indeed, many parks report record attendance during past few years. In 2018, annual attendance at parks operated by the National Parks Service hit an amazing 338 million visits – the highest level ever in more than a century of record-keeping.

But with so many sights and given most national parks' distance from major population centers, how can visitors be sure they'll make the best use of their time and see all of the highlights?

Unfortunately, many park visitors treat a national park like a drive-through restaurant. Fully experiencing any national park, though, requires that you "get out of the car." As W.H. Davies once wrote, "Now shall I walk/Or shall I ride?/'Ride,' Pleasure said; 'Walk,' Joy replied." A day hike can deliver the joy that each park offers.

What is (and isn't) a National Park

Often local tourism agencies and business groups will refer to the "national park" near their community. If you've done any amount of traveling, such statements on websites and brochures would lead you to believe that there are hundreds of national parks!

The truth of that matter is that many of those agencies and hometown boosters actually are referring to units administered by the National Park Service. The park service oversees more than 400 units, of which only 61 are actually national parks.

The types of units the park service manages are broken into more than 20 categories. Among the more common ones are national historical parks, national historic sites, national monuments, national memorials, national military parks, national battlefield parks, national battlefield sites, national preserves, and national reserves.

Other agencies also run parklands set aside for public use. The U.S. Forest Service overseas national forests. States and counties typically manage what are smaller versions of national parks and national forests. The U.S. Fish and Wildlife Service handles wildlife refuges while the Bureau of Land Management is in charge of wilderness areas.

As national forests and state parks adjoin national parks, travelers may not know when they've entered one unit or left another. Sometimes these different units even are operated as a single park, as is the case with the array of public lands protecting redwoods in northwestern California, to save costs.

National parks generally are considered the crown jewels of the park service's outdoor experiences. When visiting a national park, though, don't discount the surrounding state parks, national forests, and other recreational areas, as they also offer excellent sights to see. They're also often less crowded than a national park.

Choosing a Park to Visit

Planning a trip to a national park isn't like going to the mall. Unless you're lucky enough to live near a national park, any trip to one will be part of a vacation for you and your family. So you'll need to choose which park you want to visit.

Your interests

Begin by asking what you'd most like to see. Do you want to watch wildlife? Experience great geological features like canyons and exotic rock formations? Of deserts, volcanoes, autumn leaves, or tropical rain forests, which most appeals to you? Are you interested in history? Was there a park you've always wanted to visit since childhood?

The quandary you'll face is that you'll want to see more than you probably have vacation time for!

Getting there

Next, decide how you'll reach the park. Many parks are remote and require driving, at least from a nearby airport. How much time you have to travel and how much money you're able to spend on transportation can help you narrow your list of potential parks to visit during a vacation.

Costs

After that, determine how much money is in your budget. The good news is that the park itself is fairly inexpensive to visit. As of press time, Congaree National Park in South Carolina and Cuyahoga Valley National Park in Ohio are absolutely free to enter while at the upper end Grand Canyon National Park charges $35 a vehicle for a week-long stay.

Sometimes fees are reduced (and even waived) for students and military personnel. Generally, the vehicle pass you purchase is good for a few days.

Many times a year, the park service offers "free entrance days." Expect the park to be crowded on those days, however, as they often coincide with holidays.

If you plan to hike national parks regularly, you should consider purchasing a National Parks and Federal Recreational Lands Pass, which will get a noncommercial vehicle plus passholder and three passengers into any national park for less than $100 a year.

Even less expensive versions of the pass are available for senior citizens, the disabled and National Park volunteers. If you visit a number of parks over several weeks, you'll definitely save on admission costs going this route.

Be forewarned that there may be additional fees if planning

to camp or to park an RV. Almost any hike that involves being part of a tour group at a major destination within a park carries a cost beyond the entry fee.

The real cost will come in lodging and food. Hotels within national parks generally are pricey while those near the park entrances only slightly less so. Camping in the park or a neighboring national forest can be a good, inexpensive option. Food also can cost a small fortune within a park, but usually there are plenty of good, less expensive alternatives in nearby communities.

When to visit

Another consideration is when you will travel. Parts of some parks – such as Rocky Mountain, Crater Lake and Yosemite – actually cannot be reached during winter as heavy snowfall closes high mountain roads. Others – such as Death Valley and Joshua Tree – are simply too dangerous to hike in the summer heat. Most parks also have a peak season in which roads, campgrounds, sites and trails will be crowded; visiting a park when attendance is low but the weather good is ideal.

The high season typically is summer, running from Memorial Day through Labor Day weekends; those three-day weekends as well as when the Fourth of July falls on a Friday or Monday, usually draw the largest crowds in a year. In hot desert areas, the high season shifts slightly, as Death Valley and Arches national parks pull more people in late spring and early autumn when temperatures are pleasant.

The ideal time to visit is the off-season just before or just after high season. This can be difficult as usually high season coincides with when children are on school vacation.

Also think about the day of the week you will visit. You usually can avoid crowds by visiting weekdays, especially Monday through Thursday, when attendance dips. On three-day holiday weekends, sometimes the adjoining Thursday or Tuesday can see an uptick as well.

The time of day also plays a role. The earlier in the morning you can get to a national park, the less congested it will be on roadways and at popular sites. Usually, park visitors make their way from the nearest hotels mid-morning to the front gates and then set off again before sunset to their lodging.

Of course, visiting during the off-season and on weekdays comes with trade-offs. The weather may be cold or extremely hot; sometimes ranger-led park programs are nil on weekdays, especially in the off-season. In addition, access to some parks can be limited depending on the season. Yellowstone, for example, closes some of its entrances during winter, as snowfall at the high elevations makes roads impassable. Other parks, such as Crater Lake, can't be reached at all during the off-season because of heavy snow.

Note that visitor centers at some parks will close for holidays, especially Christmas.

Another possibility for avoiding crowds is to visit national parks that see low attendance overall. Yosemite, Yellowstone, the Grand Canyon and Cuyahoga national parks typically boast the highest attendance so definitely will be crowded during the high seasons. Great Basin (in Nevada) and Theodore Roosevelt (in North Dakota) national parks, however, are easy to reach but see few visitors compared to those in California, Arizona and Utah.

Pets

Pets are an important member of many families, and a vacation with them at a national park is possible, albeit with limitations.

Dogs and cats typically are only allowed in the park's developed areas, such as drive-in campgrounds and picnic areas, but rarely on trails. They also must be on a leash as well.

So if heading on a day hike, what to do with Rover or Queenie? Some parks offer kennels; short of that, one of your party will have to stay behind with the pet.

National forests surrounding the national park usually have more lenient rules regarding pets, so if camping you may want to consider pitching a tent there, though an adult mem-ber of the party still will have to stay with the dogs while ev-eryone else hikes the national park.

Getting Kids Involved

Children obviously can benefit from visiting these great outdoors treasures. A trip to a national park will give any child fond memories that will literally last a lifetime. During their visit, they will experience their natural joy of discovery, certainly by seeing and exploring the sights themselves or perhaps through a touch table in which they get to feel fossils or a rabbit pelt at a visitor center. The visit alone will encourage their appreciation for nature. Take them on a hike through these wild areas, and they receive the bonus of exercise in the fresh air.

The National Park Service offers a variety of great, interactive programs aimed at teaching kids about nature through fun and adventure. They often become the more memorable moments of a park visit for children, and a few even give cool souvenirs at the end.

Among the programs:

• **Junior Ranger** – Most parks now offer some version of this program, in which kids by filling out a self-guided booklet and sometimes performing volunteer work can earn a Junior

Ranger patch or pin among other goodies.

- **Ranger-led activities** – Park rangers often host family-friendly activities on the park's geology, wildlife, ecology, history and other topics. Some parks during the evening provide programs in which kids can sit about a campfire and learn about nature.
- **Star parties** – Several national parks, especially those that are remote, offer nighttime viewings of the sky with telescopes. Your kids never will see a sky so brilliantly lit with stars.
- **Touch programs** – Some parks provide kids the opportunity to meet live animals or to touch cool found objects, such as turtle shells, feathers and rocks. They usually are held at the park's nature or visitor center.

Kids' activities aren't limited to just inside the park, however. Before even leaving on your trip, have your children:

- **Check out the park's website** – Many of the websites list activities specific to their park that later can be played on the drive to the park or during hikes.
- **Meet Smokey Bear virtually** – Younger kids can learn about forest fires and nature at Smokey Bear's official website: *www.smokeybear.com/kids*
- **Visit Webrangers** – Get kids excited about your trip with a stop at the Webrangers website (*www.nps.gov/webrangers*). Kids can play more than 50 online games that allow them to explore various national parks.

Hiking National Parks Tips

Day hiking usually isn't as simple as throwing on one's tennis shoes and hitting the trail. While that may be fine at a small city park, doing so in a national park can invite disaster. Though day hiking hardly requires as much gear or planning as a backpacking trip, you still need to bring some equipment and to think ahead.

Following these 10 simple guidelines should ensure your day hike is problem-free:

- **Know where you're going** – Look at a map of the trail before heading out on it. Bring a paper map and compass with you on the trail and check both frequently as you walk.
- **Get the right footwear** – If your feet hurt, the hike is over. Good-fitting hiking boots almost always are a must on wilderness trails while cross-trainers probably are fine for paved surfaces; sandals almost always are a no-no.
- **Bring water** – You'll need about two pints of water per person for every hour of hiking and even more if in hot or dry climates. Leave soda and sugary fruit drinks at home; they are no replacement for water.
- **Layer your clothing** – Doing so allows you to remove and put back on clothing as needed to suit the weather. Make sure the layer next to the body wicks moisture away from the skin while the outer layer protects against wind and rain.
- **Carry a first-aid kit** – A small kit that allows you to bandage cuts and that contains some emergency equipment such as matches and a whistle will suffice for short hikes.
- **Don't overpack** – A lighter backpack always is better than one full of stuff you don't need. At the same time, don't skimp on the essentials.
- **Use a trekking pole** – Unless the surface you're on is absolutely level, you'll find a walking stick helps reduce fatigue. This is especially true if you're carrying a backpack.
- **Follow the rules of the trail** – Leave no trace by not littering ("Pack out what you pack in.") and by staying on the trail. Don't deface rocks or destroy signage.
- **Don't forget a snack** – Trail mix as well as jerky can help you maintain energy on the trail. It's also a good motivator for

any children with you.

• **Enjoy the journey** – Reaching the destination is never as important as having a good time on the way there. If with children, play games, pause when something grabs their attention, and never turn the hike into a death march.

Services and Amenities

Services and amenities at national parks can vary greatly depending on the number of visitors and the part of the park you're in. You almost always can expect to find a visitor center and campgrounds with bathrooms; that doesn't mean there will be a restaurant or a vending machine with snacks and water on site, however.

If hoping to stay in a park lodge or at a campground, quickly make reservations; the same goes for hotels, motels and campgrounds near the park. A safe bet to ensure that a reservation can be made is make them at least six months ahead and up to a year in advance at the most popular parks.

Most parks have at least some trails available for those with disabilities to traverse. Be aware, however, that these trails may not head to a park's top sights.

Best Sights to See

Which national park trails offer the best vistas? Lead to awesome waterfalls? Let you see wildlife? To enjoy fall colors? Here are some lists of the best national park trails for those and many other specific interests.

Beaches

Come summertime, there's almost no better place to be than the beach. The warmth of the sun upon your face, the sound of waves splashing against the shore, the blue water stretching into the horizon...

Among the most beautiful beaches you can visit are those in national parks. Thousands of miles of shoreline around lakes and along oceans are protected in our parks, and just like the wildlife and rock formations you're apt to find in most of them, the beaches won't disappoint either.

Here are six must-see beaches at our national parks.

Ocean Path Trail, Acadia National Park: Cobble beaches and hard bedrock make up most of the shoreline for the Atlantic Ocean that surrounds the Maine park's many islands. A rare exception is the 4.4-mile round trip Ocean Path Trail that heads from a sand beach to sea cliffs.

Convoy Point, Biscayne National Park: This boardwalk trail is flat and easy, running along the Florida mangrove shore known as Convoy Point. You'll follow the blue-green waters of Biscayne Bay and be able to spot some small, mangrove-covered islands. Bring a lunch; there's a picnic area below palms overlooking the bay. Part of the boardwalk also takes you out over the water. As the bay is shallow and quite clear, you'll have no trouble spotting the bottom.

Swiftcurrent Lake, Glacier National Park: The first 0.6 miles of the trail at this Montana park heads through an evergreen forest with several short spur trails leading to beaches along Swiftcurrent Lake. Meltwater from Grinnell Glacier feeds the lake, making for an crystal clear albeit cold water.

Leigh Lake, Grand Teton National Park: Several alpine lakes perfect for a family outing sit at the Wyoming park's central String Lake Area. The 1.8-mile round trip trail heads around a shimmering blue lake through green pines with gray Mount Moran soaring in the background. During summer, enjoy a picnic on the beach and then a swim in the cool waters.

Ruby Beach Trail, Olympic National Park: The Washington park's Pacific Ocean shoreline features gushing sea stacks, piles of driftwood logs, and colorful, wave-polished stones. To enjoy all three, take the 1.4-mile Ruby Beach Trail. Some of the driftwood here has floated in from the distant Columbia River.

Coastal Trail, Redwood National Park: With more than 40 miles of pristine Pacific Ocean coastline, the northern California park is the perfect place to see tide pools and sea stacks. The latter are visible from many highway vistas but to get close up to a tide pool – a small body of saltwater that sustains many colorful sea creatures on the beach at low tide – explore the 1-mile segment (2-miles round trip) of the Coastal Trail at Enderts Beach south of Crescent City.

Fall colors

Ah, autumn – the world appears to have been repainted, as red, gold and sienna orange leaves contrast with the blue sky. For many travelers, fall is their favorite time to hit the road.

But there's more to see than the leaves. As they fall to the ground, the landscape opens up, allowing you to spot interesting geological features or terrain that summer's green foliage keeps hidden. More animal sightings also are possible as birds migrate while mammals gorge in preparation for winter's cold.

America's national parks offer a number of great places to experience autumn's beauty. And with summer vacation over, many of the parks will be less crowded.

Six national parks particularly deliver great autumn experiences for travelers.

Cuyahoga Falls National Park: Brandywine Falls ranks among the most popular of the Ohio park's several waterfalls. The area surrounding the falls is gorgeous in October beneath autumn leaves, and the Brandywine Gorge Trail to it is shaded

Cedar Creek and Abbey Island at Ruby Beach, Olympic National Park.

almost the entire way by red maples and eastern hemlocks. With a combination of segments from the Stanford Road Metro Parks Bike and Hike Trail, the gorge trail loops 1.5 miles to the falls then back to the trailhead with several crossings of Brandywine Creek.

Great Sand Dunes National Park: Most people visit this Colorado park for the sand dunes soaring 60-plus stories in the sky. There's more to the park than dunes, though. The Montville Trail provides an excellent sample of that as it heads into the surrounding mountains. The 0.5-mile loop partially runs alongside a creek, where the golden canopy of cottonwood and aspen trees sends you to an autumn wonderland.

Great Smoky Mountains National Park: The 1-mile round trip Clingmans Dome Trail heads to the highest spot in the national park and Tennessee. Autumn leaves on the road to Clingmans Dome usually change about mid-October, offering a spectacular red, orange and yellow display. At the dome's top, views of those swaths of harvest colors can stretch for up to a hundred miles in all directions.

Hot Springs National Park: Though hardly thought of as a backcountry wilderness experience, the Arkansas park does offer a number of forested trails to enjoy. The best in autumn is the Hot Springs Mountain Trail. Heading through a beautiful mixed hardwood and pine forest, the route offers a gorgeous fall leaf display – and cooler temperatures than during muggy summer.

Shenandoah National Park: Spectacular autumn views await day hikers on the Stony Man Trail, a segment of the Appalachian National Scenic Trail. At the trail's top, you'll be rewarded with an expansive view of the Shenandoah Valley and the Massanutten and Allegheny Mountains beyond, their trees alit in harvest colors, as you breathe in clean, crisp air.

Death Valley National Park – OK, there are no autumn leaves here at all – but September's cooler temperatures ensure you actually can step out of an air conditioned vehicle for much longer than a minute to experience the forbidding desert landscape. Among the best places in the California park to visit is the Golden Canyon Interpretive Trail, where you can learn to read rocks that tell the tale of how a lake once here vanished.

Romance

What are the most romantic places in the world? Paris? Hawaii? Italy?

Try a national park.

Though national parks often are thought of as places to get back to nature, they're also great spots to get a little closer to your sweetie. Among the romantic possibilities are moonbows, romantic vistas, desert oasis and incredible sunrises.

Ofu Island beachwalk, American Samoa National Park.

Moonbow over waterfalls: At night during a full moon, moonbows often can be seen over waterfalls as the silvery light from Earth's nearest heavenly body refracts off the mist. Plan a spring or early summer visit to Yosemite National Park when the moon is full. On a clear night, moonbows – the moon's light reflected off water droplets – can span 2425-foot high Yosemite Fall with a trail leading right to its base.

Secluded beach: A South Pacific romance along a tropical, white-sand beach awaits day hikers on American Samoa National Park's Ofu Island. The Ofu Island Beachwalk Trail stretches about 2.5 miles one-way. As a beachwalk, there's no marked trail. The beach is a long, curve of palm-fringed white sand that feels soft and warm on the feet.

Breathtaking vistas: For many, vistas of the Blue Ridge Mountains rank among the nation's most beautiful natural

Sunrise at Pu'u'ula'ula Summit, Haleakalā National Park.

scenery. The 4-mile hike up to the summit of Old Rag Mountain via the Ridge Trail at Shenandoah National Park is challenging, but the 360 degree view from the top is unparalleled, as nearly 200,000 acres of wilderness stretch below you. Twirl your beloved around in a dance so that the entire scene spins before her eyes.

Stargazing: Boasting among the darkest skies in continental America, you can see up to 7,500 stars with the naked eye – nearly four times more than is typical in a rural area – at Bryce Canyon National Park. The Piracy Point Trail, a half-mile round trip from Far View Point, leads to a picnic area overlooking a cliff perfect for stargazing. Study up on the names of a few stars in the night sky and point them out to your sweetheart.

Fruitpicking: The Park Service at Capitol Reef National Park maintains more than 3,100 trees – including cherry, apricot, peach, pear and apple – in orchards planted decades ago by Mormon pioneers. For a small fee, park visitors can pick the fruit when in season. While there's no designated trail, the Historic Fruita Orchards Walk takes you through the fruit trees near Utah Hwy. 24. Share with your beloved what you've picked at your next rest stop.

Sunrise to propose by: At 10,023 feet, Pu'u'ula'ula Summit at Haleakalā National Park offers what many consider the world's most romantic sunrise. As the sun ascends over a blanket of clouds below the summit, it colors the crater from the inside out in an incredible light show. Bring a breakfast picnic and as the new day begins, propose marriage, for the sunrise symbolizes the dawning of your life together. Since you can drive to the summit, after she says "Yes," together hike one of the trails into the crater (either the Keonehe'ehe'e Trail or the Halemau'u Trail).

Sunrises and sunsets

Nothing quite so effectively displays Mother Nature's beauty than a sunrise or sunset, those few moments each day when the world shines golden and with incredible serenity.

Some of America's best sunrises and sunsets can be seen in her national parks. They range from the where the morning light first touches America each day to romantic sunsets over tropical waters, from the subtle signal for a million bats to begin their day to incredible sunrises over the continent's deepest chasm.

Here are seven must-see sunrises and sunsets at our national parks.

First sunrise at Acadia National Park: Day hikers can walk to one of the first spots where the sun touches America each morning via the South Ridge Trail in Maine's Acadia National

Park. The trail is a 7.2-miles round trip to the top of Cadillac Mountain, which is the highest summit on the Eastern seaboard. Though the hike would be done in the dark, with moonglow and flashlights, the trail is traversable. Acadia's ancient granite peaks are among the first places in the United States where the sunrise can be seen. Be sure to bring a blanket to lay out on the cold rock and take a seat looking southeast.

Gold-lined paths at Bryce Canyon: Fairyland really does exist – it's smack dab in southcentral in Utah, where a maze of totem pole-like rock formations called hoodoos grace Bryce Canyon National Park. Hoodoos are unusual landforms in which a hard caprock slows the erosion of the softer mineral beneath it. The result is a variety of fantastical shapes. Take the Queens Garden Trail, which descends into the fantasyland of hoodoos. When hiking during the early morning, sunrise's orange glow magically lights the trail's contours.

Bat show at Carlsbad Caverns: About 1 million Mexican Freetail bats live in Carlsbad Caverns. During the day, they rest on the ceiling of Bat Cave, a passageway closed to the public. At sunset, to feed for the evening, the bats dramatically swarm out of the cave in a tornadic-like spiral, their silhouettes stretching into the distant horizon. An open-air amphitheater allows visitors to safely watch the bats' departure in an event called The Night Flight. The Chihuahuan Desert Nature Trail, a half-mile loop, also allows you to watch the bats disperse across the New Mexican desert.

Breathtaking light show at Grand Canyon: Among the Grand Canyon National Park's most spectacular sights – sunrise and sunset – can be seen within walking distance of Grand Canyon Village in Arizona. While the South Rim Trail extends several miles along the canyon edge, you only have to walk to Mather Point, where views of the canyon shift like pictures in a

Hoodoo rock formations at Bryce Canyon ampitheater.

marquee at both sunrise and sunset. Another great spot that's a little less crowded is Ooh Ahh Point on the South Kaibab Trail, which is east of the village and south of Yaki Point. The aptly named Ooh Ahh Point is less than 200 feet below the rim.

100-mile views at Great Smoky Mountains: You can enjoy views of sunrises and sunsets with rays covering up to a hundred miles on the Clingmans Dome Trail in Great Smoky Mountains National Park. How incredible are the sunsets? They can be crowded, as those hoping to photograph the stunning scenery line up 45 minutes before the sun descends.

Romantic sunsets at Biscayne National Park: A full 95 percent of Florida's Biscayne National Park sits underwater, a turquoise blue paradise laced with vividly colored coral reefs – and nothing quite says romance like a sunset over this tropical ocean. Adams Key offers a quarter-mile trail from the dock through the hardwood hammock on the island's west side; most of the route skirts the beach, where the sunset can be enjoyed.

Needles aglow at Canyonlands National Park: Clambering over boulders and ambling across strangely angled slickrock – and watching needles aglow at sunset – await on Canyonlands National Park's Slickrock Trail in southeastern Utah. The 2.9-mile loop trail generally follows a mesa rim. Plan to walk the trail about an hour or so before sunset; on the final mile, tall thin rock formations called needles fill the horizon, glowing crimson as the sun sets.

Vistas

Certainly the best memories of any trip are the great vistas enjoyed along the way. For some, the beauty of the natural scene before them ranks far above any man-made art. For others, the diminutiveness experienced upon seeing an incredible panorama is a spiritual moment.

America's national parks fortunately preserve the most impressive of these vistas. Some offer dramatic desert scenes of changing rock colors while others deliver awe-inspiring autumn rainbows of leaves. One even lets you gaze into an otherwordly basin of hot springs.

Great Smoky Mountains National Park, Clingmans Dome: You can enjoy views of up to a hundred miles atop one of the highest points east of the Mississippi River. The 1-mile round trip Clingmans Dome Trail heads to the highest spot in Great Smoky Mountains National Park and Tennessee and the third tallest east of the Mississippi. The top rewards with an incredible 360 degree panorama. A verdant spruce-fir forest sits at the ridge tops while in autumn the leaves of hardwoods below adds swaths of harvest colors. On clear days, 100-mile views are possible.

Grand Canyon National Park, South Rim: Perhaps the

South Rim, Grand Canyon National Park.

most fantastic vista in all of North America is the Grand Canyon's South Rim. Indeed, the Grand Canyon rightly defies description. Most who see it for the first time say it reminds them of a majestic painting, appropriately suggesting it's a place that only can be visualized by actually gazing at it. While the South Rim Trail extends several miles along the canyon edge, a short section east of the El Tovar Hotel offers the best views. You'll be able to see the Colorado River a mile below and an array of incredible buttes, towers and ridges and that stretch up to 10 miles away to the canyon's other side.

Yosemite National Park, Yosemite Valley: Two sweeping views of Yosemite Valley await on the Sentinel Dome and Taft Point Loop. Located south of the valley along Glacier Point Road, the trail runs 4.9-miles. Taft Point allows you to get right up to the edge of the valley rim, offering magnificent views of

Yosemite Valley below and Yosemite Fall (the tallest in North America) and El Capitan across the way. The 360 degree views from the top of Sentinel Dome – which peaks at 8127 feet – are the hike's highlight. Among the visible sights are Yosemite Valley, Half Dome, El Capitan, Yosemite Falls, North Dome, and Basket Dome.

Yellowstone National Park, Fairy Falls Trail: The multicolored Grand Prismatic Spring and an array of geysers can be seen on the first 0.6 miles of Yellowstone's Fairy Falls Trail. A 400-foot stretch of the trail appropriately known as Picture Hill provides a grand vista of the spring. About 370 feet in diameter, Grand Prismatic is the largest hot spring in the United States and the third largest in the world. It reaches a depth of 121 feet. Be sure to bring polarized sunglasses. By wearing them, you can see the spring's rainbow colors reflected in the steam rising off the water. The smaller Excelsior Geyser Crater sits beyond the geological wonder.

Zion National Park, Canyon Overlook Trail: You can hike past hoodoos to a vista that affords a fantastic view of Zion National Park's famous Beehives, East Temple, the Streaked Wall, and the Towers of the Virgin, on the Canyon Overlook Trail. The 1-mile round trip of pinnacles, arches and domes feels like a walk on an alien world straight out of a science fiction film. Summer temps are cooler in the morning and late evening.

Mesa Verde National Park, Park Point: Park Point, Mesa Verde's highest spot at 8572 feet above sea level with 360 degree views, is often touted as the most impressive vista in the United States. The 0.5-mile round trip Park Point Overlook Trail takes you to the view of Montezuma and Mancos valleys, and on a clear day, you can see four states – Colorado, Utah, Arizona and New Mexico. Add 0.5-miles round trip to the fire lookout tower for additional great views.

Yosemite Falls, Yosemite National Park.

Waterfalls

Nothing quite demonstrates the awesome power and beauty of Mother Nature like a waterfall – hundreds of gallons of water rushing several stories over a cliffside, the vertical stream nestled in lush greenery, the mist and droplets that splash on you at the fall's base.

Fortunately, several of our national parks preserve many of the country's most fantastic falls. Most of them are quite easy to reach via short hikes.

Yosemite Falls: If there is one waterfall that everyone absolutely must see, it's this one in California's Yosemite National Park. Actually consisting of seven waterfalls, Yosemite Falls sends water rushing 2,425 feet downward into the valley. Depending on snow melt, the falls' peak flow typically occurs in May when up to 2,400 gallons of water flow down Yosemite Falls every second.

You can hike 1.2-miles round trip to the base of North America's tallest waterfall. During spring, you may want to take the trail on a clear night when the moon is full, especially if on a romantic trip. Moonlit rainbows – called moonbows – span the waterfalls.

Queenie and Fido also can enjoy the waterfalls, as leashed dogs are allowed on the trail. Be sure that your dog is comfortable with crowds and other people, however.

Tokopah Falls: Not many travelers have heard of Tokopah Falls, but it's an incredible sight. A series of cascades, it drops 1200 feet – almost the height of the Empire State Building – at California's Sequoia National Park. It's a park of tall trees and tall waterfalls. A glacier carved Tokopah Valley, leaving high gray cliff walls that cradle a meadow, creeks, and a pine and fir forest. The 3.8-mile (600 foot elevation gain) Tokopah Falls Trail leads to its namesake, which is the park's highest waterfall.

Avalanche Lake waterfalls: With melting glaciers and high mountains, waterfalls can be found aplenty in Montana's Glacier National Park. Melting glaciers feed several lakes across the park, including Avalanche Lake. Start on the Trail of the Cedars then turn off onto the Avalanche Lake Trail. The 4.7-miles round trip (505-foot gain) trail heads to Avalanche Lake, where several waterfalls from Sperry Glacier drop several hundred feet to fill the valley with its turquoise waters.

Hidden Falls: You can enjoy this waterfall and then a vista at 7200 feet elevation on Grand Teton National Parks' Hidden Falls-Inspiration Point Trail. The trail runs 3.8-miles round trip into Cascade Canyon. Though technically not a waterfall but a series of cascades running 200 feet over several multiple steps, Wyoming's Hidden Falls still impresses. Because only part of the cascades are steep, there's a lot of confusion among various sources about exactly how high the drop that looks most like

Hidden Falls, Grand Teton National Park.

a waterfall actually is – some say 80 feet and others say 100. Afterward, visit Inspiration Point, a short walk from the falls.

Fairy Falls: The trail to Fairy Falls at Yellowstone National Park offers a three-for-one deal: the multi-colored Grand Prismatic Spring, an array of geysers, and a 197-foot waterfall. If going to see Old Faithful, this is a perfect nearby trail to hike the same day. The 5.6-mile hike begins with geysers then arrives Grand Prismatic Spring, a wonder that boasts multicolored rings of algae. Fairy Falls comes next. The waterfalls' base supports a variety of vegetation. If looking for a place to picnic, the rocks downstream from the falls where raspberry bushes grow makes a perfect spot.

Marymere Falls: A trail through a lush, old growth forest that ends at this waterfall will delight anyone hiking the Marymere Falls Trail at Olympic National Park in Washington. The 1.6-mile round trip trail really is like taking two entirely different hikes in one. Most of the trail heads through an intensely green Pacific Northwest rain forest while the last portion at the destination is purely about the waterfalls. Marymere Falls is about 90 feet high, and you'll get really close to it as the trail passes the small plunge pool. Hikers also can take a stairs to see the falls' upper segment. A few landings on the stairs offers fantastic views of the falls from different angles.

Laurel Falls: Though Rainbow Falls is the tallest at Great Smoky Mountains National Park, many visitors pass it up because of the strenuous hike. One that's much easier to reach and still spectacular in its own right is 80-foot Laurel Falls. The Laurel Falls Trail runs 2.6-miles round trip through a pine-oak woods with hemlock and beech along the stream, making for a colorful walk in autumn. May also is impressive, as mountain laurel blooms along the trail and near the falls, which runs its highest that month. Deer, often with fawns, wood squirrels, and songbirds are common on the trail. The waterfall on Laurel Branch consists of an upper and a lower section. A wide walkway crosses the stream where the mist from the falls roils overhead.

Brandywine Falls: This 65-foot waterfalls awaits visitors on the Brandywine Gorge Trail at Ohio's Cuyahoga Valley National Park. The Brandywine Gorge Trail loops 1.5 miles to the falls then back to the trailhead with several crossings of Brandywine Creek. The area surrounding the falls is gorgeous in October beneath autumn leaves, but the trail can be hiked any season. It's shaded almost the entire way by red maples with eastern hemlocks and green moss upon the ground once closer to the falls.

Wildflowers

From rare California poppies to sweet-scented phlox, wild-

Catawba rhododendron blooms, Great Smoky Mountains National Park.

flowers begin to bloom each spring across much of the country. Filling green meadows, desert basins, and forest floors, wildflowers bring a special beauty that usually can only be seen for a few weeks.

Our national parks rank among the best places to enjoy wildflowers. As those parks cover wide swaths of protected land, they offer ample area for massive blooms, enhancing the already beautiful scenery.

Here are six not-to-miss spots at our national parks for spotting wildflowers from March through summer.

Pinnacles National Park: Each spring, brilliant orange California poppies, lavender-colored bush lupine, and white mariposa lilies blossom across the nation's newest national park. To see a variety of them at different elevations and from a number of vistas, take the High Peaks and Bear Gulch trails.

Great Smoky Mountains National Park: About the same time on the other side of the continent, the forest floor on the Mingus Creek Trail turns fragrant with the pleasant sent of blue phlox. Several other shade-loving flowers also can be found along the creek, including violets, Virginia bluebells and white trillium. During late April, expect to see flame azalea in bloom on the Deep Creek/Indian Falls trails. In May, look for mountain laurel, and in June for rhododendron.

Glacier National Park: From late June through early August, summer wildflower blooms are at their peak. Check out the Swiftcurrent Lake Loop Trail for meadows strewn with purple asters, white torch-shaped clusters of beargrass, and sun yellow glacier lilies, all with majestic mountains as a backdrop.

Sequoia National Park: Next to the world's largest trees are blossoms that somehow manage to stand out despite their comparative size. On the Crescent Meadow Trail in early July, lavender Mustang clover with yellow centers look like little pins of brilliant light against the immense pine cones that have fallen into the grass.

Crater Lake National Park: Wildflowers usually bloom along the stream next to the Annie Creek Trail and across the meadows from mid-July through August. Among those that might be spotted are Macloskey's violet, big huckleberry, sulphur flower, Crater Lake currant, western mountain ash, and wax currant.

Great Basin National Park: Amid the high desert is an oasis of summer wildflowers on the Alpine Lakes Trail. Spring-fed Lehman Creek flows into a lake and supports Parry's primrose, penstemon, and phlox, all set against vibrant green grass. Butterflies are abundant here as well.

Wildlife

America's national parks are known for their great vistas and fantastic rock formations, but they also preserve another treasure: wildlife.

Bison at Lamar Valley, Yellowstone National Park.

In fact, national parks rank among the best places to see interesting and rare wildlife. Late summer marks a particularly good time for wildlife viewing at many parks as most mothers bring out their young that time of the year.

Given the breadth of national park locations, there's also the opportunity to see almost every kind of North American wildlife, from those that live on mountains, in marine environments, and in the tropics to those that make their homes on prairies, deserts and in temperate forests.

Mountains: Travelers can explore the "Serengeti of North America" on the Lamar Valley Trail at Wyoming's Yellowstone National Park. Like the mountain-ringed African plain, Lamar Valley serves as home to the classic megafauna that define North America. Bison, elk, grizzlies, black bears, wolves, coyotes, eagles, osprey and more all can be found at this high elevation. Coyotes also can be seen wandering about, looking for a meal while bald eagles and osprey grace the skies. Grizzlies reside in the hilly woods, but they and the area's other big two predators – black bears and wolf packs – prefer to remain under cover than be seen.

Marine: You can encounter an array of marine wildlife on the Beach Trail at Alaska's Glacier Bay National Park. Low tide also provides an opportunity to see intertidal life. As the waters retreat into the ocean – and water levels here can fall 25 vertical feet, among the greatest extremes in the world – a number of animals and plants are exposed. Don't be surprised to spot starfish and snails on the sands and grasses. On shore, a variety of sea birds gather and fly over, often nabbing exposed intertidal creatures for a meal. During those first moments of sunlight, watch for humpback whales, harbor porpoise, puffins, sea otters, and Steller sea lions, frolicking and feeding in the mouth of the bay. Bring binoculars. If lucky, you'll also hear the blow of humpback whales.

Tropics: Tropical wildlife can be safely seen from the Anhinga Trail at Florida's Everglades National Park. The trail's boardwalk takes you over open water where you can watch for alligators peeking out of a river, as well as turtles, herons and egrets. Winter marks the best season to see the most wildlife. A number of birds spend their time in the Everglades after migrating from a northern clime. Among those you can spot are the double breasted cormorant, great egret, great blue heron, snowy egret, tricolored heron, white ibis and woodstork. Turkey vultures congregate in the marsh during the early morning hours.

Prairies: North America's largest mammal – the bison – freely roams North Dakota's Theodore Roosevelt National Park, and the Buckhorn Trail is an excellent place to spot them and other Great Plains wildlife. The trail includes a prairie dog

Gila woodpecker, Saguaro National Park.

town that stretches for about a mile. You'll be able to spot them barking from their burrow entrances as they keep an eye out for predators. Hawks, coyotes and rattlesnakes are among the creatures hoping to make an unsuspecting prairie dog its dinner.

Deserts: Four desert ecosystems can be found in North America, and the park closest to a major metro area offers among the best spots to see wildlife of these dry climes. Outside of Tucson, Ariz., Saguaro National Park's Douglas Spring Trail crosses the Rincon Mountain District (Saguaro Park East), providing the chance to see coyotes, roadrunners, jackrabbits, quail and Gila woodpeckers. All five of those creatures thrive in the Sonoran Desert, which stretches across Arizona and northern Mexico, as well as good portions of the continent's other three desert ecosystems.

Temperate forests: Great Smoky Mountains National Park, though stretching across the Appalachian Mountains, offers the opportunity to see many of the animals that reside in temperate forests covering much of the continent east of the Mississippi River. The Deep Creek/Indian Falls trails in the park's North Carolina section sports Eastern cottontail rabbit, groundhogs, river otter, and white-tailed deer. Also present but much more elusive, as they keep to themselves, are black bear, bobcat, coyote, red fox, red wolf, and wild boar.

Winter

Most travelers think of summer as the best time to hit national parks – but winter also offers several spectacular sights that make for memorable visits.

So when the snow starts falling, consider a road trip to one of the following parks.

Birders paradise: Winter marks the best time to hike Florida's Everglades National Park, as the subtropical climate means unbearably hot and buggy summers. Indeed, a number of birds already know this and spend their time in the Everglades after migrating from a northern clime. Among those you can spot on the Anhinga Trail are the double breasted cor-

Golden Canyon, Death Valley National Park.

morant, great egret, great blue heron, snowy egret, tricolored heron, white ibis and woodstork; turkey vultures congregate during the early morning hours.

Wildlife sightings: Leafless trees and snow's white backdrop makes sighting large wildlife a lot easier in winter than summer. The Warner Point Nature Trail on the south rim of Colorado's Black Canyon of the Gunnison National Park offers the chance to spot elk and Rocky Mountain bighorn sheep. Look for the elk in clearings and the bighorn sheep on the rocky cliff sides.

Heavy waterfalls: At most parks, waterfalls are most active in spring and early summer, thanks to snow melt. Not so at Washington state's Olympic National Park. Rain is more likely there during winter, meaning the water flow is higher, making for a more spectacular creeks and falls. One good trail through the park's lush, old growth forest that ends at a waterfall is the Marymere Falls Trail.

Bearable heat: During summer, oppressive heat makes California's Death Valley National Park at best a pass through seen from a motor vehicle. The park's average high in January is a pleasant 67 degrees, though, making winter the perfect time to walk the foreboding desert landscape. Among those sights is the lowest point in North America. Badwater Basin sits 282 feet below sea level and can be accessed in a mile-long round trip hike.

Avoid the crowds: Visitation drops during winter at most parks, so the trade-off for bundling up in coat, cap and gloves is seeing the great scenery without all of the crowds. A good bet is Yosemite National Park's spectacular Yosemite Valley in California. The Lower Yosemite Fall Trail offers a number of fantastic views of Yosemite Falls in a 1.2-mile loop with the added coolness of falling water frozen in mid-flight on the granite rocks.

Christmas

A little secret: Among the best ways to escape holiday stress is a national park trip. Only a couple of the parks close in winter, and almost all offer warm, cozy and peaceful holiday experiences. A bonus is that almost all parks are less crowded during winter.

Here are five great holiday-themed must-do's at our national parks.

Winter wonderland, Yellowstone National Park: Book a getaway at the Old Faithful Snow Lodge, which can only be reached this time of year by snow coach or snowmobile. The Christmas-decorated lodge keeps its fireplace burning with plenty of hot cocoa for visitors. During the day, hike past "ghost

Christmas caroling in the cavern, Mammoth Cave National Park.

trees," formed when the steam from the Old Faithful geyser freezes on pine tree needles. Bison with snow-covered manes often feed across the geyser valley.

Polar Express train ride, Cuyahoga Valley National Park: Each December prior to Christmas, the Cuyahoga Valley Scenic Railroad's Polar Express chugs through the scenic Ohio park. Among the highlights on the refurbished passenger train is a reading of the children's book "Polar Express," which inspired a movie and this trip. Many passengers ride the train in their pajamas! If in the Southwest, a private company also runs a Polar Express to Grand Canyon National Park.

Luminaria-lit skiing: Denali National Park: Every December, rangers light the small paper lanterns that line ski trails at the Alaska park. Visitors also can snowshoe or stroll the route, which leaves from the Murie Science and Learning

Center, Denali's Winter Visitor Center. Several other National Park Service sites offering luminaria displays and hikes including Florida's De Soto National Memorial and Arizona's Tonto National Monument.

Snowshoe wildlife hike, Rocky Mountain National Park: Ranger-led snowshoe tours take visitors of this Colorado park to a variety of wildlife, including elk, coyotes, deer and snowshoe hares. The trail is utterly quiet as snow-capped mountains and evergreens rise around you on all sides.

Caroling in a cave, Mammoth Cave National Park: In early December, the Kentucky park holds Christmas carol sing-ing in the world's longest cave system. It's a tradition that goes back to 1883 when local residents held the first Christmas celebration in the cave's passageways.

Historical sites

While the National Park Service's 61 major parks largely focus on protecting natural wonders and wilderness, they also preserve several historical sites. Though many are merely ruins, others are in just as good of shape (if not better) than when they originally stood.

Historic Fort Jefferson: At Dry Tortugas National Park, you can visit a fort used during the Civil War. Built with more than 16 million bricks during the mid-1800s, Fort Jefferson is the Western Hemisphere's largest masonry structure. Six walls and towers with a moat make up the fort's outer area on Garden Key.

19th Century Mining Town: Crossing a thick rolling woodland, the Colorado River Trail at Rocky Mountain National Park offers nice views of Colorado River, arguably the Southwest's most important waterway. The trail to the ruins of an 19th century mining town, Lulu City, in a 6.2-miles round trip with 320-

John Oliver cabin in Cades Cove, Great Smoky Mountains National Park.

foot elevation gain.

Appalachian life: A number of great day hikes allow visitors to explore the Great Smoky Mountain National Park's rich history. Pioneer cabins and mills await on several short day hikes, including those at Cades Code and Mingus Mill.

Butterfield Stage station: Along the Texas-New Mexico border, you can step back into the Old West and experience the remoteness of what once was a welcome sign to travelers: a Butterfield Stage station in the Guadalupe Mountains. The 0.75-mile round trip Pinery Trail marks a great day hike for families at Guadalupe National Park. The trail leads to the ruins of the Pinery Station, a once favored stop on the original 2,800-mile Butterfield Overland Mail Route.

Trees

Among the most fantastic sights at our national parks are

trees. Whether they be gigantic, fossilized, or older than the hills (figuratively speaking), they're certain to awe. Here are six great tree sites to visit.

Sequoias: Your family will feel like hobbits walking through scenes from "The Lord of the Rings" movies on the General Grant Tree Trail at Kings Canyon National Park. The 0.5-mile trail heads through the General Grant Grove of giant sequoias. More than 120 sequoias in the grove exceed 10 feet in diameter and most tower several stories over your head.

Redwoods: Hiking families can enjoy a trip into what feels like the forest primeval on a segment of the Damnation Creek Trail in Redwood National Park. For those with younger children, a 1.2-mile round trip through just the redwoods section of the trail makes for more than an incredible, inspiring walk.

Bristlecone pines: On several of Great Basin National Park's glacial moraines rise incredibly ancient bristlecone pines, many nearly 5,000 years old, meaning they began growing as the ancient Egyptians built the pyramids. The 2.8-mile round trip Bristlecone Pine Trail allows you to walk among a grove of the trees, which scientists say likely are the oldest living organisms on Earth.

Old growth forest: The largest expanse of bottomland hardwood forest in the southeastern United States can be found at Congaree National Park. It includes several champion trees, including a 36-story high loblolly pine. Hike the 2.4-mile Boardwalk Trail loop to see bald cypress, tupelo and more.

Chestnut trees: Day hikers can head through what used to be a grove of majestic chestnut trees. Great Smoky Mountains' Cades Cove Nature Trail runs 1.4-miles round trip trail (from the parking lot) and sits in Cades Cove, an isolated mountain valley that is a popular destination thanks to many well-preserved structures from pioneer days. A few seedlings of the

Base of General Grant Tree, Kings Canyon National Park.

great chestnut remain.

Petrified forest: Families can hike the remains of a woodlands dating from the dinosaurs' earliest days on the Great Logs Trail in Petrified Forest National Park. The fairly easy walk consists of two loops that combine for a 0.6-mile round trip. Because of the hot Arizona weather, spring and autumn mark the best time to hike the trail.

Learn more about these and many other great national park trails in the author's **Best Sights to See at America's National Parks**.

About the Author

Rob Bignell is a long-time hiker, editor, and author of the popular "Best Sights to See," "Hikes with Tykes," "Headin' to the Cabin," and "Hittin' the Trail" guidebooks and several other titles. He and his son Kieran have been hiking together for more than a decade. Rob has served as an infantryman in the Army National Guard and taught middle school students in New Mexico and Wisconsin. His newspaper work has won several national and state journalism awards, from editorial writing to sports reporting. In 2001, *The Prescott Journal*, which he served as managing editor of, was named Wisconsin's Weekly Newspaper of the Year. Rob and Kieran live in Wisconsin.

CHECK OUT ALL THESE GREAT HIKING BOOKS BY THE AUTHOR

"Best Sights to See" series:
- America's National Parks
- Great Smoky Mountain National Park
- Indiana Dunes National Park
- Joshua Tree National Park
- Rocky Mountain National Park
- Voyageurs National Park

"Hikes with Tykes" series:
- Hikes with Tykes: A Practical Guide to Day Hiking with Children
- Hikes with Tykes: Games and Activities

"Headin' to the Cabin" series:
- Day Hiking Trails of Northeast Minnesota
- Day Hiking Trails of Northwest Wisconsin

"Hittin' the Trail" series:
National parks
- Grand Canyon National Park (ebook only)

California
- Palm Springs and the Coachella Valley

Minnesota
- Gooseberry Falls State Park
- Split Rock Lighthouse State Park

Minnesota/Wisconsin
- Interstate State Park
- St. Croix National Scenic Riverway

Wisconsin
- Barron County
- Bayfield County
- Burnett County (ebook only)
- Chippewa Valley (Eau Claire, Chippewa, Dunn, Pepin counties)
- Crex Meadows Wildlife Area (ebook only)
- Douglas County
- Polk County
- St. Croix County
- Sawyer County
- Washburn County

GET CONNECTED!

Follow the author to learn about other great trails and for useful hiking tips:
- Blog: *hikeswithtykes.blogspot.com*
- Facebook: *dld.bz/fBq2C*
- Pinterest: *pinterest.com/rbignell41*
- Twitter: *twitter.com/dayhikingtrails*
- Website: *dayhikingtrails.wordpress.com*

If you enjoyed this book,
please take a few moments to write a review of it:
smile.amazon.com/dp/1948872080

Thank you!

CPSIA information can be obtained
at www.ICGtesting.com
Printed in the USA
LVHW082143221222
735827LV00029B/815